Journey into Childhood

Also by Lois Lenski

Journey into Childhood

The Autobiography of Lois Lenski

J. B. Lippincott Company

Philadelphia   New York

U. S. Library of Congress Cataloging in Publication Data

Lenski, Lois, birth date
  Journey into childhood.

Autobiography.

I. Title.
PS3523.E575Z5   813'.5'2 [B]   74–141451
ISBN–0–397–31177–X

To my
beloved grandchildren

Blessed Lord of Word and World
Who givest us our days,
May daily work my worship be,
My daily joy my praise.

CONTENTS

FOREWORD

This book is a journey, a journey backward into my own childhood, to the childhood of children in my family, into childhood of the past and of the present, as reflected in my books. It is not a strict autobiography, for it is concerned only with those biographical details which have a direct bearing on my creative life and work.

An autobiography is a confession, not to a kindly priest in confidence, but to the public. Over the years I have been asked many questions about my background and its effect on my work; how, when, where, why. . . . This is my answer. I hope it will show the relation between the creative person and the creative product.

We look upon the present day as a time of great change. And yet the eternal verities are the same yesterday, today, and tomorrow. They do not change. Children in all ages have the same loves and hates, the same joys and fears, the same laughter and tears. In any age and in any environment, children show the same courage, resilience, and stoicism. A mother braiding a child's hair, a boy catching a ball, a girl petting a cat—these gestures are eternal, common to all humanity. There may be some variation in pattern, but they all say the same thing. Childhood is preparation for living.

My own childhood has been given back and relived through the lives of my son and the other children in my family, and through the lives of the children of past and present, about whom I have written. It is my hope that my books have enriched the lives of the children who are my readers.

Lois Lenski

A Girl to Her Favorite Author

O you who write my dearest books,
I wonder if you knew
That I would steal away
Alone to quiet secret nooks
Where I could weigh
Your every word
And dream about it too.
I wonder if you thought of me,
O you who wrote my books.

I wonder if you struggled hard
And if your hopes came true.
I wonder all about your life,
Your joys, your friends, your looks,
I wonder if you longed for fame,
As other people do.
I wonder if you thought of me,
O you who wrote my books.

Mary Scott
Whittier, California
1950

Journey into Childhood

CHILDHOOD

SPRINGFIELD, OHIO 1893–1899

My paternal grandfather, William John Lenski, was Polish, and was born in Passenheim, East Prussia, Germany, in 1837. My paternal grandmother, Ernestine Louise Pittlekow Lenski, was Russian, and was born in Boblitz, West Prussia, in the same year. My father, Richard Charles Henry Lenski, and his brother Paul, were born in Greifenburg, Prussia, in 1864 and 1866. The family came to this country in April, 1872, and settled in Jackson, Michigan. Grosspapa Lenski was a tailor by trade.

My mother, Marietta Young, was born in Franklin County, a few miles south of Columbus, Ohio, in 1863. Her mother, our "Grandma Young," was a widow, her husband, William Young of British ancestry, having died before their youngest child was born. My mother had a brother, Edwin A. Young, "Uncle Ed," and a sister, Wilhelmina Young (Kuhlman), "Aunt Willie." Grandma lived in a log cabin and did truck gardening to educate her children.

Grandma's grandfather, Philip Helsel (or Heltzel), of Pennsylvania Dutch ancestry, was one of the first settlers in the Sciota River valley, south of Columbus. He emigrated from York County, Pennsylvania, with his wife, Mary Willis Helsel, and eight children, to Ohio in 1808. The first Lutheran church was organized in his barn near Valley Crossing. He is buried in the Valley Crossing cemetery. (My book, *A-Going to the Westward,* is dedicated to him and his wife.)

My father was sent from Jackson, Michigan, to Capital University, the Ohio Synod Lutheran College and Seminary, at Columbus, Ohio, for his education. There he met my mother, and married her on February 1, 1888.

I was born October 14, 1893, in Springfield, Ohio, and was given the Bible name, *Lois,* with the middle name *Lenore.* At this time my parents were living at 422 Cedar Street, but shortly after my birth, they moved to the parsonage at 416 West Columbia Street, where I spent my first six years. My father was minister of Zion Lutheran Church from 1892 to 1899.

My earliest memories are very hazy and are mixed up with the photographs my father took, and also with tales told by my older sister and two older brothers. I was the fourth of five children. Esther was the oldest, five years older than I, then Gerhard and Oscar, myself, and Miriam, the youngest. In 1896, when I was three years old, I had *membranous croup,* and my life was despaired of. This was described as "a membrane growing over the windpipe," and they had to keep me inhaling steam day and night, which was not easy without electricity. There was no antitoxin, no antibiotic for babies at that time. At the same time, my brother Oscar came down with scarlet fever, so we had two quarantine signs on the front of our house, and no one could come in. People walked by on the other side of the street, holding handkerchiefs over their noses. Mrs. Theodore Hax, a member of the congregation, stayed with us and helped my mother take care of us by day, while my father took the nights.

It was Mrs. Hax who had saved my life. I acquired a sort of halo, a reflected glory for not having died. I was so good as

14

to be almost angelic, because, I suppose, of my close brush with Heaven. But I am afraid I got over it speedily and my earthly nature began to assert itself. On my parents' tenth wedding anniversary, in 1898, they took a trip to New Orleans to see Mardi Gras, and in their absence, Grandma Young came to take care of the five of us children. On a certain day, so the story goes, Grandma wanted me to take castor oil and I refused. She promised me a nickel if I would take it. I took the nickel—but still refused the oil! Ever after that I was called "stubborn."

We had a small yard in Springfield, big enough for a bed of cannas in the front, and an array of cacti in pots on the front porch. In the back yard there were a few trees, a small barn for our horse Bill and the phaeton, and a large cold frame for cacti. My father was a man of many hobbies and his interest in cacti, canaries, and photography had already begun. A photograph shows his five children admiring the cacti in the cold frame and another standing behind a large canary cage, on legs, which held about twenty birds. The picture must have been taken on Sunday, for Esther is wearing her new broad-brimmed leghorn hat trimmed with lilacs, of which she was very proud. Another important member of our family was Joe Bill Maltese Hopfoot Kitty Lenski, our cat. Oscar claims to have invented the name, which was used for many succeeding cats in our lives.

My father was also interested in pencil sketching, and filled several sketchbooks with drawings of his children in all sorts of activities. That he had a definite urge toward artistic expression, there can be no doubt. I marvel now to think of the originality of my father's ideas. Not many men, with a large city congregation to look after, two or more sermons to preach on Sunday, pastoral work, theological study and conferences, work with church organizations, and other duties would have taken the time or had the inclination to do such interesting things with his five children.

His first camera was a small one, but he took many fine

photographs with it. I still have a photograph of his night-blooming cereus, whose midnight blooms each June attracted a crowd of neighbors and townspeople to our front porch. We children were photographed in a variety of poses. There is one picture of me, holding some fuzzy baby chicks on my lap. I well remember when it was taken. I have a very unhappy look on my face—and for good reason. My dress was clean and I didn't want any droppings on it!

My father's photographs record both the exterior and interior of the house on West Columbia Street. The parlor had a large bay window with an oleander, a rubber tree, and a pomegranate, as well as ferns, palms, geraniums, and other potted plants. Above them hung several small wire cages filled with canaries. My mother was a keen gardener all her life and dearly loved her plants.

The house had two fireplaces with small shiny glazed horizontal tiles, and mirrors over ornate mantelpieces, on which sat various vases and statuary. On one stood a bust of Martin Luther at one end, Beethoven at the other. One of my father's most fascinating photographs was a view of himself looking in the mirror above one of those fireplaces. He took it by means of a long cord attached to the shutter of his camera, an ingenious device he had worked out. The photograph showed both back and front views of his head. He wore a mustache at this time with long whiskered ends, although still a young man.

Minnie Marks, a "hired girl," stayed with us while Miriam was a baby, as my mother was not well. Another child was born that died, and Mama's health did not improve. The doctor said that she must stay outdoors, but he would not allow her to do gardening, as it would tire her too much. So Papa bought a horse and buggy and Mama took long drives. All her life she talked about the Texas pony she had owned when she was teaching school south of Columbus, before her marriage. Now again she had a horse to enjoy. Once she drove to Middletown, where her sister, Wilhelmina Kuhlman, lived.

Esther went with her and it took all day. My father's photographs show many views of my mother, a graceful young woman, riding horseback on a sidesaddle. She used to go out to the Kemler farm and some of the Kemler young people rode with her. One photograph shows me as a child of four being pushed in a rope-swing by Clara Kemler, then in her teens.

A strange memory lingers. Once I saw my mother cry—and my whole world tumbled. I was upset for days, not knowing, not understanding. . . .

Grossmama and Grosspapa Lenski came from Michigan to visit us once in Springfield. From the pictures, Miriam and I look to be about three and five. We wore terribly plain, austere dresses and our hair was braided back tight in a succession of little braids, the ugliest style imaginable. It was certainly not flattering, and must have taken hours to do up. But, of course, it stayed in perfect shape all day long. Not a single hair could get loose.

There is a picture of me sitting on Grosspapa's lap on the front porch of the parsonage. I look quite serene and happy, although I was never quite comfortable in Grosspapa's presence. I remember Grossmama as being very warm and affectionate, especially to her son Richard (my father) whom she adored, and whom she had "given to the Lord," but Grosspapa always seemed cold and cynical to me. I was always afraid he would laugh at me, although he never did. Perhaps it was just innate Lenski dignity.

Helen Clark, a girl of my own age, lived two doors away. She had a large collection of dolls of all kinds and kept them arranged neatly on a wide windowsill. She was an only child and much petted.

We had good neighbors in Springfield. The Nagels lived a half block away on the corner. Their yard had a grape arbor and an ornate "summerhouse" with vines. With them lived their nieces, Catherine and Elizabeth, and the crippled nephew, Conrad, in a wheelchair. Will Nagel shared my father's hobby of photography and other interests. They kept up a close friendship and visited us often in later years. The Margileths lived across the alley from us. Ella Bockway was another devoted friend. She was a German teacher in Springfield High School, was in and out of our house a great deal, and visited us later in Anna. She always dressed in the latest fashion and I looked up to her in awe and admiration, although I was a bit afraid, too. She gave us a Ping-Pong set one Christmas and each year some of our loveliest books. Once she went to France and brought Miriam and me little French boy dolls which we treasured.

We moved from Springfield to Anna, Ohio, on October 9, 1899, when I was six. My mother often mentioned the date and I have never forgotten it. Mama was reluctant to go, for she loved Springfield and the advantages of city life. A farewell party was given for us on the eve of our departure. There was a big crowd of people, I sat on a fat lady's lap and kept sliding off. That night I slept in a strange house, separated for the first time from my little sister and my mother, and I was bitterly homesick. I could not eat and I had a frightening nightmare, seeing a window full of outstretched hands, unexplainable and terrifying. Finally I cried myself to sleep.

We were given farewell gifts, Papa a pair of red satin suspenders embroidered with flowers, which he never wore, but which reposed in the bureau drawer in the spare room for many a long year. Mama received an ivory fan with ostrich feathers which was to keep the suspenders company. The large crayon portrait of Papa, a previous gift from the Springfield ladies, went along too. We took the cat, Joe Bill, in Mama's covered pattern basket, along in the train with us. At the very last minute, somebody brought Miriam a present—a red tin horse on a base with wheels. Everything was packed, so Papa hastily tucked it into the big empty canary cage. The cage, with the tin horse standing upright inside, caused a minor sensation when it was hauled down Main Street to the parsonage in Anna, in Chris Fenneman's dray.

My second book, *A Little Girl of 1900*, gives a fictionized account of my actual memories of Springfield.

ANNA, OHIO 1899–1911

Arrival Anna was a small town in western Ohio, with a population of only two hundred, but when the new Lutheran preacher arrived with his wife and five children, it increased to two hundred and seven. We moved by train, chartering a freight car for our household goods. I remember nothing about the trip except that we had to "change cars" somewhere.

And then, after a long and tedious ride, we were there. To us, the new town looked very strange.

> "What a funny little depot, with no big roof at all, and only a big round stove and two or three benches. What strange people to shake hands with—and strangers standing on street corners staring, or looking out of windows. What a funny muddy street and what funny little stores and houses."*

It seemed a long walk to the new home. Once there, we forgot how tired we were, as we explored it from top to bottom. Miriam and I ran all over the house. The windows were very tall and narrow, but had wide windowsills. With Helen Clark's windowful of dolls in mind, we shouted, "Mine! Mine! This windowsill is mine!" as we came first to one, then to another. It seemed a wonderful house to have so many windowsills!

The first days and weeks were chaos and confusion. The furniture came, was unloaded and carried in. Carpets were tacked down, boxes and barrels unpacked. Beds were set up, furniture arranged, and pictures hung. Then suddenly the emptiness disappeared and it began to look like home.

Anna, Ohio, in the early 1900's was a perfect child's town. It offered all a child could enjoy and comprehend. Common-

* *A Little Girl of 1900.* Stokes-Lippincott, 1927.

place and ordinary, it had no particular beauty or grace, but it soon became my own, a compound of sights and sounds and smells and buildings and people that became a part of me. It was a horse-and-buggy town, automobiles being yet in the future, and life moved at a slow pace. Telephones were of the wall type, and I suppose we had one, but I do not remember ever using it. The most familiar sounds were the whistles of a train passing through, the *clop-clop* of horses' hoofs on the dirt streets, the barking of dogs and the ringing of the church bells. These sounds were, a half-century later, the symbols of a vanished way of life. To have lived it and savored it and been a part of it, has given me great comfort through ensuing years.

It was not long before I knew every house and who lived in each, and could stop and talk at every gate, or running by, call hello. It was not long before I knew every building and street and back alley and tree and bush and yard and fence as well as I knew my own. There was always some errand to take a little girl down the street. Coming from the parsonage, I turned the corner at the Lutheran church—first a white frame building and later the large red tile-roofed brick of which my father was so proud. Just beyond it stood Doc Harbour's office, a separate building beside his house with its wide front porch. I came to know the inside waiting room, too, its walls lined with hundreds of photographs of babies the doctor had brought into the world.

In the next block was the fire station, jail, town hall, several other buildings, a saloon, and then Woehrle's Grocery at the corner. How often I ran in that door, asked for a pound of Arbuckle's XXXX coffee, then called, "Charge it!" and dashed out again. Whatever we bought was charged and my father paid the bill at the end of the month, bringing home a big sack of hard candy for a special treat.

Across the street Louie Stork had an ice-cream parlor, and on the two other corners were imposing brick mansions, built by wealthy retired farmers. Farther up the street beyond the livery stable was Weller's drugstore, with pretty colored bottles in the windows, and still farther on, Finkenbine's Department Store. In one half, millinery and drygoods were sold, in the other half, groceries. The display windows were always exciting. Miriam and I would press our noses to the glass, saying: "I'll take that!" "I'll take that!" choosing objects on display—purses, handkerchiefs, or hats that we would buy if we were rich, a favorite game of ours. It was a favorite store and we loved it.

On the other side of the street near the hotel was the post office, where Bobby Martin's father was postmaster and where the Lenskis' box No. 3 was always crammed with mail. From here, we children could take a shortcut through vacant lots to the school on the back street. Across the railroad tracks stood the big grain elevator, opposite the undertaker's establishment. The depot was right beside the tracks of the Cincinnati Hamilton and Dayton railroad, C. H. & D. to us, an intriguing place from which one embarked on travels to see the world, or where we went to welcome visitors from far away. Passenger and freight trains puffed through the town, with mournful, long-drawn-out whistles.

Once there was a train wreck not far from town, and after most of the debris had been carried off, we searched the tracks and found pieces of broken mirror and fragments of drapes which we took home for our dolls.

In the spring, boys in overalls and girls wearing sunbonnets carried tin buckets and picked strawberries among the cinders along the railroad tracks a mile or so from town. Passengers often waved to us, and sometimes even the engineer and conductor.

My little sister Miriam never picked many strawberries. She would stand and eat, then ask us to help her fill her bucket. Esther and the boys were good pickers and I did fairly well myself. Once we had a rattlesnake scare. I still get cold shivers when I hear that awful rattle. We never saw the snake, we always ran too fast. Worst of all—an anticlimax to our day—

was the long, hot trudge home. Mama wanted the berries and made them into delicious jam.

Of course we knew all our neighbors. Louella Brideweser and her mother lived in the house north of us, and Grandpa and Grandma Woods beyond them. On up the street lived the Hensels and down by the pond where we skated, the Jenkinses. Across the street opposite us, in a small boxlike house, with only one outside door, Doc Steeley lived. He was a bachelor and did no doctoring. Once his sister and little niece came to visit him from Florida and told us of all its wonders. Down at the corner, opposite the church, lived old Mr. and Mrs. Kah, and their daughter, Lena, the church organist.

Odd characters were often seen on the streets. Some lived in town, like the harmless half-wit on the hill and certain drunks who staggered in and out of the two local saloons. Others appeared from nowhere, transients who came and went, probably hopping freight trains on the C. H. & D. railroad. Tramps were common, appearing unshaven and shoddy at the back door, asking for food, sometimes offering to work. The scissors-grinder, with his grindstone strapped to his back, and the umbrella mender were always welcome. Now and then an organ grinder with a monkey appeared, and all the children in town followed in his trail. Book agents were common. They sold, or tried to sell, Bibles, encyclopedias, or histories of the world.

Gypsies sometimes passed through town. Once we heard that a band of gypsies was camping in a field not far away. The town children had a great fear of them and our friends told Miriam and me that they liked to steal children. Our father took us to see them and we held tightly onto his hands. We looked into the swarthy faces, lit up by bright eyes and dangling earrings. We liked the full colorful skirts and gay colored shawls around their shoulders. To our astonishment, we saw that they had children, too!

The town that looked so commonplace and unpromising at first improved with time.

"The next day and the next and the next and a great many more were spent in getting acquainted. The people who looked so strange on that first day suddenly became friends and dropped in to help and visit. The muddy streets and grassy sidewalks turned into familiar pathways. The little stores were places of enchantment where we ventured alone without the protecting nearness of Mother. The fields and meadows and orchards and vacant lots were unexplored kingdoms of thrilling adventure. The neighbor children turned into the most enterprising and satisfying of companions. And the funny little houses and the church and the stores turned into one's own dearly loved town."*

The Anna House   The Anna house was the first of three remarkable houses in which I have had the good fortune to make my home. The first two were so remarkable as to be fantastic, like the wildest dreams of absurdly impractical architects. The third was remarkable for its age and beauty.

The Anna house was like none other in the world. What a wonderful house it was, and what a perfect place for children! It had steep gables and peaks and small porches, long narrow windows and a winding stairway. The porches and gables were ornamented with gingerbread trim, jigsaw scrolls, fancy pilasters and balustrades. The house was built in 1882 by German carpenters who were artists in expressing themselves in the medium of wood. Although it was ugly by some standards, the house had a look of repose and homely elegance about it.

Actually, it was an awful house, a preposterous house, from a woman's point of view—no electricity, no gas, no furnace, and as inconvenient as possible. My mother cordially hated it. For years she dreamed of the glories of city life left behind in Springfield, and it was only her sense of humor that enabled her to adjust. The house had an unheard-of number of outside doors—was it twenty-one? Papa said it was a big job

* *A Little Girl of 1900.* Stokes-Lippincott, 1928.

to lock up at night, and Mama laughed about it for years. I don't think anybody ever really counted the doors—we just enjoyed the exaggeration. There were, at any rate, far too many.

But for the children it was wonderful, a perfect house made just for us. It was full of mystery and magic, inside and out, and we never ran out of ideas. There were places to climb, places to hide, and even though the yard was a tiny one, there were all kinds of places to play, trees and fences and ladders in the barn to climb. And not in the yard only. We could always spill over into alleys and dirt streets and vacant lots, and even into the fields and woods beyond.

The house sat inside a picket fence with a gate. The click of the latch gave warning that someone was coming in along the winding herringbone brick sidewalk. The parlor bay window jutted out in front, and over it was a tiny upstairs porch with an ornate balustrade; and behind, a door and two windows into "the little front room" which Esther had to herself. In front of the bay window was my mother's flower bed, planted each spring with pink vincas and purple verbenas. A purple clematis vine climbed up a trellis to the roof of the study porch. Along the alley fence was a bed of roses and at the corner a huge clump of pampas grass, with great feather dusters on top when it came into bloom.

On the right by the alley was the big old apple tree, with a tree-house in its branches, where Esther piled up pillows and read by the hour in hidden secrecy. Underneath was the wooden lawn swing swaying back and forth, full of happy children playing *Train,* and lustily calling out the names of all the stations along the line: *"Lima, Wapakoneta, Botkins, Anna, Sidney, and Piqua! All aboard!"*

To the left of the bay window was the larger of the front porches, the only one large enough for the whole family to sit on at once, and crowded at that. Its door opened into my father's study, and this entrance was used largely for church callers. The porch on the right side was smaller and had two doors, one into the parlor and one into the sitting room. Here entered all the family visitors, and here we children ran in and out. Still farther to the right, the dining room also had a front door, not often used, but kept open always on hot summer days for ventilation.

The house was always a busy place, with plenty of activity flowing over into the yard. The picture was never the same, but was always changing as the hours of the day passed one into the other.

It was a happy home, buzzing with comings-and-goings, and all the excitement and drama of family living.

Inside the House   The sitting room was the heart of the house. It was never called the living room. The main source of heat in the house was the big base-burner against the inside wall. It had small isinglass windows on three sides through which you could watch the flames within. There was a fancy ornate chrome top which you had to push to one side. Then you lifted the coal bucket and poured in hard anthracite coal. You could rest your cold feet on the shiny fenders at the side, to warm them.

In the center of the room stood the chenille-covered table with the large kerosene lamp, which threw dark shadows across the carpeted floor. Around this light we clustered to read or study each night after supper in the cold months. Papa and Mama sat reading in comfortable rocking chairs. The *Cincinnati Times-Star* was our newspaper. Miriam loved to take down Mama's hair, and, standing on a footstool behind, comb and brush it and pin it up in curls and puffs and braids. Mama said she found it restful. After school work was done, we played games—no playing cards (they were wicked!) but flinch, or dominoes, or parchesi. My father was a great chess player, but alas! none of his children learned to play.

After games, Papa would pull out his watch and say, "Time for bed, children." We rose dutifully to kiss our parents good night. "Good night, Mama." "Good night, Papa." Each in

25

turn. A light kiss for each. We were never demonstrative and this was about the only time we kissed. The door to the hall and stairs always stood open for us, and up we would go, passing a hat-stand and an umbrella rack there in the hallway. Up we would go, clinging to the curving banister, the same banister worn slick from our many down-slidings!

Some alterations were made in the house before we left it, but I remember it best as it was at first. Back of the sitting room was the dining room, almost filled with a big dining table with many "leaves"—a new one had to be put in when "company" or Grandma came—and a small sheet-iron stove beside the sideboard. There was also a glassed-in cupboard for Mama's good dishes. She had a special set of Haviland china of which she was very proud.

Before a meal we always said grace. Grace meant "asking a blessing." After the meal, we "returned thanks." Each night after supper, we had family worship. My father read from the Bible, spoke a prayer, and we all prayed the Lord's Prayer together.

Behind the dining room and down two steps was the old kitchen on the alley, with coal and wood-burning range and what we called the "sink." This was a homemade cupboard, with a recessed counter of zinc, on which I washed dishes in a tin dishpan. There were shelves below for pots and pans and a bin at one side for a fifty-pound sack of flour. In the corner was a closet for groceries and supplies, which was also used as Papa's darkroom for photography.

The kitchen range had a reservoir for heating rain water. On top stood a singing teakettle to keep the kitchen moist and humid. There was a large oven for Mama's homemade bread and rolls, for her cakes, cookies, gingerbread, and pies. She liked to bake bread on ironing day, when she kept up a good fire to keep the irons hot. The warmth in the kitchen helped the yeast to rise. There was a huge copper clothes boiler, used to boil the white clothes on wash day, and a big griddle for frying buckwheat pancakes. We ground our coffee in a wooden coffee mill. How often I sat on a chair and held it between my knees, turning the grinder by hand. It had to be freshly ground for each meal, to make the best coffee.

The floor of the kitchen was wooden boards, oiled, without linoleum. We girls took our turns scrubbing it with scrubbing brush and yellow soap, on our hands and knees, each Saturday. It was a task to keep it clean. The kitchen was the scene not only of hard work, but of plenty of fun, too. Here we popped corn, made taffy, and greased our hands and pulled it. Here we cracked hickory and black walnuts on a flat-iron with a hammer, or froze homemade ice cream in a freezer turned by boy-power. Here, in later years, we made fudge and fancier candies—fondant and bonbons and chocolate-covered peanut clusters.

For years, Miriam and I always washed the supper dishes, to music, our own music. We sang duets while I washed and Miriam dried. We sang all our school songs, including *Poor Pussy* and *I'm a Gypsy:*

> " 'I'm a gypsy,
>   Oh, I am a little gypsy girl!
>   The forest is my home
>   And there I love to roam,
>   For I am a little gypsy girl!' "

We were afraid of gypsies in real life, but we loved to sing about them.

Ohio has always been noted for its good food and its wonderful cooks. My mother was no exception. Although she was not German herself, she could match the best of the German farmers' wives, whose real artistry lay in the foods they prepared. We three girls all learned to cook and to cook well. Our mother never set out to teach us. She never said, "Now I want you to learn to cook." We were always in the kitchen helping and we learned without realizing it. We did whatever Mama did. I slipped up on two things—dressing a chicken and making pie-crust. Esther or Mama always dressed the chicken or made the pie. I never had a chance, but had to teach myself, after I was married.

The kitchen was the scene of all our ablutions, and especially of baths on Saturday night. Rain water was heated in the reservoir and in kettles. It was warm and cozy in the kitchen, even on cold winter nights. We climbed in the big tin tub, one after the other, under Mama's supervision, in the dim light of a kerosene lamp with a reflector hanging on the wall. Once Miriam and I were having our baths on a Saturday afternoon, with the window shades securely pulled. A farmer, bringing something to the parsonage, walked down the alley, came into the woodshed and opened the back kitchen door. We thought the door was locked, but it wasn't. Bath time was about the only time we locked any doors. He poked his bearded head in and withdrew it quickly. I'm sure his face was red!

Our doors were left open all day long, but my mother never got used to having people walk in without knocking. She had to put up with it because it was the custom.

My mother's life could not have been easy, with all the cooking, all the sewing (she made clothes for all of us, even suits for the boys) and all the washing, besides gardening, shopping, and many other tasks. The only outside help she had was from Mrs. Adams, a Negro woman, who came to do the family washing every Monday, somewhat irregularly, for she had a large family of her own. The water was heated on the range, and carried to tubs on benches on the brick porch. One tub held hot water and had a washboard for soaping and rubbing. The other held cold water, for rinsing and bluing the clothes. Then they had to be run through the attached wringer. When Mrs. Adams was not there, Esther fed the clothes in, while Miriam and I took turns turning the wringer. In wintertime, the clothes were frozen stiff on the clothesline, and one's fingers tingled to take off the clothespins and pile the stiff pieces in the basket. They melted in the warm kitchen, to be only half-dry; then they could be rolled up without dampening, ready for ironing.

I never did much ironing, because Mrs. Adams or Mama or Esther was there to do it. This was another chore I somehow escaped. Oh—I could iron after a fashion, but my heart was never in it!

The parlor was a sacred spot, for here were our finest possessions. It was not a cheerless and gloomy room, but gay, colorful, and inviting. Double sliding doors led into it from the sitting room, and a single door from Papa's study. The thick Brussels carpet had a large flower pattern and the wallpaper was covered with brilliant curlicues. There was a mantel without a fireplace under it, on which stood Papa's eight-day marble clock which had to be wound only once a week. The windows had folding inside shutters and long, starched lace curtains reaching from the high ceiling to the floor. The furniture was a "parlor set" with cushioned settee, platform rocker, and several straight-backed upholstered chairs.

In the middle of the room was a small, square, marble-topped table with a beautiful lamp, whose globe-shaped base and shade were decorated with red roses. The table held our family Bible in which births and deaths were inscribed in my father's careful handwriting. We loved to look at our names in a row and the dates of our births. There were also two plush photograph albums, one red and one green, with photographs of Mama and Papa when young, our grandparents and strange relations we had never seen. Papa's crayon portrait stood on its white and gold easel in one corner, with a white tasseled silk scarf or "throw" draped artistically over the top—the gift of the Springfield ladies.

On one wall hung a large chromo of "The Burning of the Books," a picture greatly prized by my father. On another hung framed photographs of the five of us and our parents taken by a professional photographer.

Many weddings took place in our parlor. Miriam and I had a favorite place to sit on the winding stairs. From there we could peek through two glass transoms and admire the beautiful bride, with the long train on her skirt. Our idea of high fashion was having a long train on your skirt. After the ceremony was over, we could take a peek around the corner of the smoke-house and see the bridal couple on the brick porch, being photographed by my father in front of a rolled-down backdrop.

My mother loved beautiful clothes and dressed in the height of fashion. With a small income of her own, she was able to buy the finest of materials and have her dresses made by a good dressmaker in Sidney. Photographs of her taken by my father testify to her beauty and to her interest in fine clothing. She dressed her children well, too, making all their clothes herself.

The Brussels carpets in sitting room and parlor presented a problem. Long before "wall-to-wall carpeting" as a commercial phrase was ever heard of, our carpets ran from wall to wall, and were tacked down at the edges, under a molding, with carpet tacks. Under them was a layer of heavy "carpet paper" to make them soft to walk on. Before the days of vacuum cleaners (we got our first one after 1911) a carpet had to be taken up and carried out of doors to be cleaned. Once a year it was hung on the clothesline or laid on the grass and pounded with a carpet beater by well-trained boys, then returned and tacked down in place again.

Oscar recalls a time when we all wanted to go to the circus in Sidney on a certain day, but housecleaning interfered. So we all pitched in and worked as fast as we could. We got to Sidney by ten o'clock the next day in time to see the parade, hear the calliope, and see the lions in their cage. That after-noon we saw the circus—we had earned it!

Not only was the carpet cleaned at housecleaning time, but everything else as well. Spring cleaning was a horrible but necessary ritual. My memories of it inspired this verse:

> *"Clean the house in springtime*
> *With a rag around your head;*
> *Scrub the windows, scrub the ceiling,*
> *Beat the mattress and the bed.*

Never mind about the family,
Pull the pictures from the wall;
Was there ever such excitement—
*No one knows the place at all!"**

Our parents slept in the downstairs bedroom at the foot of the stairs, while we children slept upstairs. There were four upstairs bedrooms, "the little front room" for Esther, "the girls' room" for Miriam and me, and "the boys' room" for Gerhard and Oscar, and in the back, a "spare room" for company. The downstairs base-burner had a drum (an enlarged stovepipe) in the room above, Miriam's and mine. This drum was supposed to heat our room, but if it did I never noticed it. In winter, our bedrooms were always freezing cold. We undressed downstairs by the stove, then made a dash for our beds upstairs, often with heated irons wrapped in newspapers in our arms, to be placed under the comforts to warm the cold mattress through and through. We wore our long-sleeved underwear all night under our flannelette nightgowns. It was the only way to sleep warm.

The bedrooms had bureaus with marble tops and large mirrors, and washstands with washbowls, pitchers, and toilet jars, but we usually washed in the kitchen, where there was plenty of warm water, and dried on the roller towel there. At night in bed, Miriam and I curled up tight together and whispered comforting words as we listened to the windows rattle in bad thunderstorms or heard the rain pounding on the porch tin roof.

Over the stair well, there was a long narrow closet, where we once went "camping out." It seems we had all decided to go camping and sleep out in the woods, but it rained and we were not allowed to go. It was Esther's bright idea that we camp out in this closet instead, and we all acquiesced. Oscar and Gerhard slept on the shelves, and we three girls on the floor. There was an anticlimax, of course. All went well until

* *Skipping Village.* Stokes-Lippincott, 1927.

the middle of the night when Papa heard some strange noises and bumps overhead, and came upstairs to investigate. The next minute we were all marched off to our beds.

This may seem like a fabrication, but it is not. The boys' initials are still on the woodwork, and on the wall is inscribed the words: "Lois Lenski slept here!" (Why they picked on me I don't know!)

Esther had other bright ideas, too, and being the oldest, had considerable power and we all followed where she led. Once her teacher at school talked about the glories of the sunrise, and asked how many of the children had ever seen it. Esther had to admit she never had, and feeling disgraced, set about to remedy the situation. That night she got us all up and led us out in the yard to look toward the east, out over the barn, to wait for the sun to come up. We waited and waited, but it didn't come. Papa came instead—and once more we were marched back to bed!

The closet downstairs in our parents' room was the place where Mama hid our Christmas presents, after returning from a mysterious all-day trip in the buggy with our horse, Pet, to Sidney. We always knew they were hidden there, so it became a place of mystery. Once Miriam and I peeked in and felt of certain bumpy packages, hidden behind a big box of scraps, trying to guess the contents, but we were too scared to open anything. Besides, we did not want to spoil our Christmas.

There was the time that Miriam's friend, Ethel Price, spoiled hers. Her mother sent her to our house each evening prior to Christmas, and this made Ethel suspicious. One night she returned home earlier than usual. She peeked in through the crack of a tightly-drawn shade and saw her mother sewing on a new red silk dress that was to be her Christmas present! Miriam and I thought this a terrible calamity—to find out ahead of time what you were going to get for Christmas. But Ethel loved to brag about it!

Ethel provided a lot of drama for us.

We well knew that Ethel, with her long black curls and big

32

black eyes, was a spoiled child. Once she came home from school, ran into the kitchen of her home and opened the cupboard door, looking for something to eat. Seeing nothing better, she grabbed the vanilla bottle and drank from it. Her mother screamed, "Ethel! That's rank poison!" but it was already down Ethel's throat. For weeks, Miriam and I watched Ethel, expecting her to drop dead any minute or at least to fall in a fit. It was years before we learned what "rank poison" was.

When Ethel heard talk of the haunted house by the school-yard, she began to brag about a coffin. We girls all crowded round to listen. She told us it was in the cellar of the house where she lived. We did not believe her, so she said she would show us. Hers was a double house, and one side near the alley was vacant. She took us down the outside cellar stairs into a dark, damp, cobwebby cellar, and sure enough, there on the shelf was a long oblong box! We did not stay long enough to investigate what was inside it. We dashed up to daylight again, convinced that Ethel had told the truth. It really was a coffin!

Miriam was almost a match for Ethel, when it came to fearless daring. Upstairs, a door from the little front room opened onto the small porch over the big bay window below. This had an ornate railing around it, but if you climbed over the railing, you could walk around on the narrow eave-ledge. Miriam did it once, when she was only four, and the whole family stood in the yard below watching, terrified. Mama was afraid to call to her for fear of frightening her and making her fall. So we all just stared up at her. Serenely she made her way around the ledge onto the roof of the little sitting-room porch, then climbed onto the over-hanging limb of the old apple tree and calmly slid down, quite surprised to see she had had an audience.

One kitchen window looked out in the alley. Across the alley, the ground rose in a slight terrace, two or three feet, topped by a rickety fence around the Demings' garden. Their yard was higher than ours and was overgrown with weeds and brush. Their big two-story-and-a-half house was almost hidden in a jungle of uncared-for bushes and trees, for both the

Demings were very old. Old Mr. Deming was a retired G.A.R. soldier, and always marched to the cemetery in the Memorial Day parade. He loved to tell of his Civil War experiences to anyone who would listen. After he died, Mrs. Deming lived alone and the place went to neglect. I remember her well, hunched and bent over, but with bright keen eyes peering out from under her sunbonnet. She had a bed of brilliantly-colored verbenas by her kitchen doorstep, portulaca by the front walk, and a large trumpet vine with red blooms obscured the front gate.

Our kitchen was only one story, with an attic loft over it, the gable end of which was open to the woodshed. There was a ladder and we could climb up. Old magazines were stored there—*The Youth's Companion, Woman's Home Companion, Literary Digest,* and others. It must have been as dark as pitch, but we climbed up there to read them on rainy days, while the rain pounded on the roof. Here, too, Miriam and I cut out dozens of paper dolls from the fashion pages. How we could see to read and cut I have no idea.

In the woodshed was a bin for hard coal, and a huge bin for corncobs and kindling for starting fires. Also rows of piled-up, chopped firewood. My brother Oscar, who was clever with tools, had a workshop in the woodshed and once made a "shocking machine" and loved to try it out on us. Miriam and I took turns. We had to grasp spools in our hands, from which wires went to the machine. When Oscar turned it on, it made a loud buzzing noise and gave us an electric shock that made us dance and squeal. I seem to remember a lot of jars on a shelf filled with liquids in different colors, too. Oscar was always up to something!

A small coalshed was tacked on behind the woodshed. There we shoveled our coal buckets full of soft coal, big lumps of which had to be cracked and split with the hatchet. Getting in wood and coal was a never-ending task in wintertime, to keep the big old house heated and comfortable.

Beside the dining room was the old "wooden porch," with the cistern of rain water below and its iron pump. We used this water to wash our hair and clothing. The wooden pump on the brick porch by the kitchen was for well water. There I pumped many a bucket of water to carry into the house. There, too, our neighbor, Louella Brideweser, coming through a side gate, filled her own buckets with water. There at the wooden pump, on cold days, my wet mittens would freeze to the metal pump-spout, and have to be torn off with difficulty. There I, or someone in the family older than I, had to pour boiling water from the teakettle down the pump, holding the handle up high in the air, to "prime" it and thaw it out. Before we went to bed on cold nights, we had to lift the handle and "let the water down," listening as it gurgled, to prevent freezing.

What a conglomeration of outbuildings on one small lot! Behind the brick porch was the smokehouse, also with a paved brick floor and a smoke chimney. We never smoked any meat, but we did hang smoked hams and shoulders there. And I recall barrels or kegs of sauerkraut and dill pickles sitting inside. The cellar entrance was outside, beyond the brick porch. How often we slid down that sloping cellar door! At the bottom of the steps inside, in the damp coolness, we kept crates of eggs, crocks of apple butter, and row upon row of canned fruits, jams, and jellies. In the section that had a dirt floor we stored root vegetables and potatoes, and had large bins for apples, especially delicious Northern Spies. At this time we got our milk for five cents a quart, and fresh homemade butter from Si Young at his farm a mile away, for twenty cents a pound. The old brick porch was a good place to play on rainy days, a good place to sit and peel apples or peaches at canning time, or to pluck a chicken to be cooked for Sunday dinner. My father also took photographs there.

This conglomeration of architecture, so many gables and roofs and porches, made an inviting place for the boys to climb. They would go up to the highest peak of all, yell down at us timid girls and try to frighten us. But they always came back down again safely.

Over by the fence in the back yard was a sweet-apple tree, with a crotch for a huge potted begonia. Beside the house by Bridewesers' fence was a sandpile where we played. Oscar made beautiful roads and bridges, and whittled diminutive telephone poles. He made little wagons out of empty cigar boxes, with slat bottoms, like real ones, for dumping sand. He let Miriam and me play with him, but he had all the ideas. A border of rosebushes lined the fence and Mama always had a bed of pansies by the woodshed. Back of the small lawn, with the clothesline, was a vegetable garden with clumps of rhubarb, raspberry bushes and sunflowers. In later years, we had the use of a lot back up the alley on a hill and grew our vegetables there.

A brick walk to the barn ran under the grape arbor, over which grew Concord grapes in profusion and provided a goodly supply of jelly each fall. (When I went back for a visit in 1961, after fifty years, I was astonished to see that the trunks of these grapevines were three inches in diameter!) At the end of the walk was the old red barn with its stable and manure pile, the outhouse and the chickenhouse and yard. There were rows of beehives, too, when my father had the bee fever. How was there space for it all on this small lot? I can still see Papa and one of the boys in their amazing bee outfits, and hear Mama pounding on a dishpan to bring back a swarm of bees that had settled in a tree. Papa's bee-keeping hobby brought strenuous drama into our lives. (I have described this in *A Little Girl of 1900*.)

The barn as we knew it was a favorite play spot for the five of us. We held pet shows there, after rolling the buggy out into the alley, and charged pins for admission. We performed acrobatic stunts on trapezes in the haymow and sometimes we climbed to the top of the roof outside and slid down on barn and stable shingles, landing in the straw-pile below, none the worse for wear.

Beloved childhood home! Not a square foot of that house or yard, not a single detail of color or pattern or object but would stay with me till my last day, so vivid are the impressions of childhood.

Small house, small yard, small town—it was a very small world to have been the center of all those activities and dramas and escapades, all those joys and delights, sorrows too, of a family of five growing children. It was a small world made luminous and beautiful, with no limitation in width or breadth, bounded only by the unfettered imaginations of five growing children. A small world, a good world, a fortunate world in which to grow up.

The writing of *Shoo-Fly Girl,* my Amish Regional, in 1962, brought back to me vivid memories of my childhood, so similar in many respects. The Amish now live much the same life that small-town and rural people in Ohio and Pennsylvania lived in the early 1900's before the advent of the automobile. In the Foreword of my book, I wrote:

> "I had identical experiences and impressions—the kerosene lamps, the wood range in the kitchen and its welcome warmth on a chilly night, the cold barn at evening lighted by dim lanterns, the milking of cows amid the smell of hay and dust, the Saturday scrubbing of the kitchen floor on hands and knees, the Saturday baking and getting ready of the children's Sunday clothes, the emphasis of religion of Sunday. . . . All these things I have seen and felt and known as a child.
>
> "The ride in a buggy behind a horse, the slapping of the lines, the horsey smell, the *clop-clop* of the horse's hoofs heard when one is lying in bed at night, the enveloping darkness in the kitchen just before the lamp is lighted, the welcome glow of light shining on little upturned faces, the dark scary shadows in the corners and in stairs and hallways. All these things I saw and sensed and felt as a child. I heard also certain words

and phrases which were once a part of the warp and woof of my daily life, expressions I had not heard for over fifty years, a heritage from early German-Americans."*

This was life as I knew it, a child in Anna.

The Lenski Family: Father   As a child, I felt that I had the right kind of a father. He always had a good supply of pins under the lapel of his coat, a sharp penknife in his pants pocket, and half-a-dozen pencils in his vest pocket. All these things came in handy when a little girl had need of them. On his desk there was a big jar of library paste, which he used for mounting photographs. That came in handy, too, especially when Papa wasn't looking.

My father's "study" was his *sanctum sanctorum.* We were allowed to come in whenever we liked, if there were no visitors, and if he was not too busy. If we saw him writing, we knew we had to be quiet. Miriam and I learned to read each other's lips across the room. Papa spent days and days writing at his desk, and we wondered what he was writing about. He never told us. His desk was a big walnut one, with drawers on two sides and a space for his legs and wastebasket between. (I still have his desk and have written many books upon it.) We loved to explore his wastebasket and salvage scraps of perfectly good paper, even the backs of used envelopes. Paper was hard to come by in those days, our other chief source of supply being the blank sheets between the cakes of shredded wheat. These were kept to draw pictures on. Besides the desk, there was a comfortable Morris chair beside the sheet-iron stove, and there were tall bookcases that reached the ceiling, four of them. On the bottom shelves of two were thick ancient books bound in white calfskin.

From my father's "study," I early got the idea that it was a good thing to have a room with a closed door to keep others out, a desk inside with plenty of pens and pencils, a place to

* Foreword, *Shoo-Fly Girl.* Lippincott, 1963.

write down what one was thinking, a place where ideas came
. . . a place to get away from others, where no one could
tease you or pester you. I knew that a study was a most de-
sirable place—but I never achieved one until years later,
after my marriage.

As a young man, my father's parents destined him for the
ministry, and out of their frugal means, sent him to Columbus,
Ohio, to the Lutheran College and Seminary at Capital University. My mother was at this time living and teaching rural
school on Groveport Pike, south of Columbus. Her brother,
Edwin Young, was also a student at Capital. Through him, my
parents met. My father was a great student. He spent long
hours at his desk, and even though surrounded by children, he
had the ability to concentrate.

Personally, while he was a serious man, he also enjoyed a
great sense of humor. He was a popular preacher, not only
because of his message, but because of what people called
his "personal magnetism." His personality made a strong appeal—his intense bright blue eyes seemed to look right through
a person. He could make a guilty individual feel very uncomfortable. He was a determined man and held fast to his
own opinions, fighting hard against his opponents or those who
differed with him. Because he had the courage of his con-
victions, he made enemies. But in spite of his enemies, there
were hundreds who loved and admired him.

My father was very strict about moral matters. He dis-
approved of dancing, card playing, drinking and drunkenness,
vice of every kind, and even of the theater, because he felt it
fostered vice. He was harsh in dealing out punishments. When
he was angry, he could strike fear into the heart of a child.
When he expected obedience, you obeyed, and instantly,
without question, delay or argument. He was cold and un-
demonstrative in affection. It was hard for him to show the soft
side of his nature. He was like his own father in this, and unlike
his warm and affectionate, outgoing mother.

He was a methodical man and followed a strict routine.

Every day at a certain hour, he walked to town to the post office to get his mail out of box No. 3, and to bring home meat and groceries for the day. He was so regular in this performance that housewives along the street would say, "There goes the preacher!" and boasted they could set their clocks by his timing. He had a regular schedule for work and for play for all the days of the week. He loved work and was never happier than when he was working. I have spoken of his hobbies, and I am sure these were his creative outlets. They were not passing fancies, as the word might indicate, but abiding passions while they lasted, and many of them lasted over a long period of years, overlapping others. Whatever he did, he did with intelligence and intensity and thoroughness. He never left tasks unfinished.

In Springfield, his hobbies were three—cacti, canaries, and photography, with sketching a possible fourth. In Anna, they were bee-keeping, raising chickens, Rhode Island Reds, and rabbits, Belgian hares, the two latter probably planned for and shared with the boys. His photography continued, always a permanent interest. After we moved to Columbus, he switched to gardening, raising gladioli, asters, and dahlias. Of all his hobbies over the years, photography was the best beloved and the most enduring. In Springfield, he shared it with Will Nagel and they learned its intricacies together. He acquired a new and larger camera with a tripod, after we came to Anna, and took much larger photographs. He did all his own developing and printing of negatives (glass plates) and pictures, and mounted them with professional skill. He had the slim, delicate hands of an artist. His darkroom was the kitchen pantry, with pots and pans moved out. I often helped him and learned the entire process myself. This was long before drugstores started a developing and printing service.

We children always made good models. My sisters and I, as we were growing up, were sure to have our pictures taken every time we acquired a new dress or a new hat. Here my father indulged his creative instincts. He planned "artistic" poses—myself with what we then called "flowing hair" (in actual life, I always wore it tightly braided!) smelling a lilac, no clothes on above the waist; vain little Miriam, also with "flowing hair," looking in a hand mirror, also waistless; Esther holding her violin at a precarious angle like a concert player. . . . There was no end to his ingenuity and invention.

The brick porch was an ideal place to pose his models. The light was probably diffused there and perfect for his purpose. He acquired professional backdrops, artistic chairs, stools, and other accessories such as were being used in photographic studios. He borrowed table covers, portieres, and sofa cushions from the house. Taking photographs with hooded camera set on a tripod, without artificial lighting, was an elaborate and exacting affair, but his results can pass muster with fine photography today. Because of his proficiency, he became the unofficial photographer for the entire area, and was soon known far and wide for his handsome pictures. Everybody came to him to be photographed—there was no competition nearer than Sidney—individuals, wedding couples, new babies, children of all ages, family parties and larger groups. The photographs he took were a social record of a rural Ohio community at the turn of the century. It is unfortunate that only a few of them have been preserved, and that all his boxes and boxes of plates were ruthlessly buried when we left Anna in 1911.

Mother My mother never knew her father, for he died before her younger sister was born. It was at a box supper in her one-room schoolhouse that she met my father. A very elegant professional photograph, taken at the time of my parents' marriage, shows them both very thin, serious, and dignified. My mother is seated, wearing a dark, shiny silk dress, the skirt of which is festooned with four tiers of white lace. It has tight sleeves, high collar with bow of ribbon, lace around bolero and at cuffs. She wears a small hat with ribbons and a plume, black gloves, and in one hand holds the handle of an umbrella.

My father wears a dignified dark suit, with a gold watch chain across his buttoned vest. He rests one hand on the back of my mother's chair, and in the other holds his bowler hat. He is bareheaded, slightly bald and has a small moustache. That they started out in life seriously there can be no doubt. By the time they reached Anna with their five children, both had changed considerably. They had increased in weight and were more mellow and lighthearted.

Although my mother had had an aversion to country life even before she married, she reconciled herself to it for the twelve years we lived at Anna. She was extremely competent in all phases of homemaking, and we three girls helped as much as we could. Some of my happiest memories are of sitting in the warm kitchen with Mama and Esther, peeling fruit for canning; or all sewing together and talking. We came closer to her at these times than at any other. After we began making our own clothes, Mama let us choose our own materials and patterns. I must have been a student in college before I ever owned a readymade dress.

As president of the Ladies' Society in the church, my mother presided with grace. This was before the days of women's active participation in community organizations. She lamented her lack of education, was determined that all her children should go to college, and often said that after she got them educated, she was going back to college herself. This desire she never realized.

Personally she was tall and handsome. She turned gray in her thirties and I remember her only with gray hair. She always dressed well and took pride in looking her best. Around the yard, she wore a "fascinator," a loosely-knit head covering, which was pretty on her soft, curly hair. In the evening, sitting by the table to read, she often wore a "shoulder shawl" with fringes, around her shoulders. She would sit, reading, with one hand raised, twisting a curl of her hair at the back of her neck. There were always curls over her collar at the back, although, of course, as in the style of the day, she wore her long hair in a high knot, pinned with hairpins and a back comb. My mother had a habit of talking aloud to herself. We would come in the room, see no one with her and ask, "Who were you talking to, Mama?" To which she would reply with a smile, "I was speaking to a lady!" Whenever we asked her how old she was, she would say, with a twinkle in her eye, "As old again as half!"

Mama had a way with horses, as I have already mentioned. Our horse, Pet, learned the trick of unhooking the stable door and leaving. She would roam all over town. If Papa and the boys went after her, she would let them almost get a hand on the bridle, then she would turn and frisk away. The harder they chased her, the faster she ran. No one could catch her but Mama. Leaving her housework, Mama would put an apple in her pocket and go off to look for Pet. She would come up closer and closer to Pet, grazing in somebody's flowerbed, offer the apple, and Pet would take a bite, then docilely follow her home.

My mother had a frugal upbringing, without a father. She constantly warned us of the sin of wastefulness. It was a sin to throw away or to waste food. "Somewhere a child is hungry," Mama often said. "If you waste food, you will go hungry yourself some day." The ladies of the church packed missionary barrels to be sent to India and China. This was a frugal period, too. Americans had not yet become "waste makers." We were taught not to waste anything. We saved string and rolled it into balls. We saved wrapping paper and used it over again. We hoarded used envelopes and backs of business letters to use for writing and scribbling. My mother and grandmother used old clothing for carpet rags, to be made into rugs.

I was frugal, too, and saved my pennies when I had any.

Spending a nickel was difficult, at the County Fair in Sidney, for instance. There were so many choices—lemonade, peanuts, ice cream, candy. I thought it over carefully and decided not to get something to eat or drink. These treats were too soon over with. No, I wanted something tangible, something to take home with me, something to last a while. I would end up by buying a handkerchief or a rubber ball on a string. Mariam did not agree. She spent her nickel recklessly for sweets and had forgotten all about it by the time she got home. But I had my rubber ball.

Our parents were quite unworldly and unmaterialistic. In the training we received from both our parents, money and the making of money were not important and were never a goal. True, it was necessary to have a certain minimum to live on, and we were taught to save and to be frugal, but money as an end was never thought of. We never bought anything on credit. We never even thought of buying it unless we first had the money in hand. We did not know the meaning of the words "installment buying." We never borrowed or went into debt. Debt was something to be abhorred. Part of this attitude is characteristic of the period, and was probably true of the majority of right-thinking people. But also, part of it was personal to my parents.

Learning was always our goal. My parents had a strong positive attitude toward learning and education. The most important thing was to *learn,* work hard and learn, read books, study . . . there is so much to learn. They stressed, not so much in words, but by example, the importance of *work.* They were not afraid of work. They believed in applying yourself wholeheartedly to the task in hand, not because you were forced to do so, but because you loved to do it. You enjoyed doing all that was expected of you, and more. You always did *more* than you were asked to do. Work was a joy and a delight. Find congenial work and do it with all your heart and soul. They set the example and we children followed. I am the product of their teaching. Work to me is sacred. I have a strong urge to work, I am not happy unless I am at work. I believe this compulsion to work was not only a part of my conscious training, but also a part of my Polish inheritance.

Grandparents My mother's mother, Sarah Young, our "Grandma," was very much a part of our childhood. At this time, she had given up her own home at Valley Crossing, south of Columbus, and lived with her three children, spending part of the year with each, her son, Edwin Young, her younger daughter, Wilhelmina Kuhlman, and Marietta Lenski, my mother. Grandma was a very independent person. She wore long black dresses with long sleeves, a bonnet on her head tied with a bow under her chin, and a shawl around her shoulders. Her eyes were keen and her face was a network of wrinkles. We never knew when she was coming or when she was going to leave. She traveled alone by train from one home to the other and would always arrive unexpectedly. Suddenly, there at the gate, Grandma would come walking in, carrying her little suitcase. We would fly out to meet her, take her suitcase from her, and drag her in. Quietly, as if she had never gone away, she fitted herself into the family routine. All we did was put an extra leaf in the dining-room table!

Grandma had reduced her earthly possessions to a bare minimum, just what she could carry with her. She never gossiped, she never told tales of what had happened at Aunt Willie's or Uncle Ed's. She was a wise woman and kept her own counsel. I am sure she was a great help to my mother, for she entered into everything. She helped with the cooking, the cleaning, and the sewing. When I was eleven, she encouraged me to piece a quilt. She helped me cut the pieces and showed me how to join the blocks together. It was the Irish chain pattern. I worked willingly at first for I liked to sew, and then I bogged down. I had not yet learned the discipline of carrying a task through to the end, so Grandma came to my rescue. The quilt would never have been finished without her help. I kept it all through my married life, a remembrance of her. I also have another, a Pennsylvania Dutch hand-woven spread in red and blue, which she had preserved over the long years.

Our Lenski grandparents visited us in Anna in 1900, when Esther was eleven. Mama was sick and Papa had to help with the cooking, something he practically never did at other times. I remember when they first arrived. Grosspapa smiled in a dignified way and nodded his head. Grossmama put her arms around my father in a close embrace, exclaiming, *"Richart, mein Sohn, Richart!"*

It was July and very hot, as only Ohio summers can be. Grossmama kept the shades in the spare bedroom pulled down during the day, to keep the room cool. This was something new to me. The room was dark and spooky when we went inside to talk to her. Grossmama always had her spectacles on and was reading the Bible. Grosspapa did not stay in the room. He sat outside in the shade of a tree, reading a newspaper. He paid little attention to us. Grossmama and Grosspapa Lenski did not enter into our daily lives as Grandma Young did. They were strangers, special guests, to be treated with great respect.

The next year, 1901, my father took Miriam and me along with him on a visit to his parents in Jackson, Michigan. Mama bought us new hats for the trip at Finkenbine's store. We took the train and had to change cars at Toledo. There we saw some boats on the river, and there the story of my un-acceptance of the word *Maumee* as a name for a river began. I refused stubbornly to believe that any river could have such a funny name as that. The story clung to me all my life. I remember little about the visit, except that Uncle Paul, Papa's brother, had baby twins at the time and how much Miriam and I enjoyed them. (A fictional account of this visit is described in *A Little Girl of 1900.*)

The Five of Us Of the five of us, each was different from the others. Our very differences made for drama in our growing up. Each child was shaped by the others into his own individuality. Esther was the oldest, in a class by herself. Gerhard and Oscar, "the boys" made a lively pair, and Miriam and I, "the girls" another. Oscar, the middle one, was often pulled both ways. Gerhard and Esther looked down upon him as a baby. But his two little sisters looked up to him and thought he was wonderful.

Esther had considerable influence over us, but was always

kindly and tolerant about it. We never resented her position, but rather admired her for her invention and ideas. When she was not coaxing us into carrying out one of her lively schemes, she was always reading. She seemed to swallow books whole, and read far more than any of the rest of us. Reading helped her to evade household chores, but she became proficient in the household arts in spite of herself. She shared with my mother a sense of responsibility for the bringing up of her brothers and sisters and was determined not to let any of us stray from the straight and narrow path. For myself, although I usually took her advice, I never felt I was being imposed upon. She and I, despite the five years difference in age, built up a congenial companionship and devotion for each other, which have lasted all our lives.

Gerhard was always the perfect gentleman. Even while quite young, he was always fastidious and a bit vain. He had a keen sense of what was seemly in public. At the age of four, in Springfield, he cried and had to be spanked every Monday morning, because he insisted on wearing his Sunday suit. This suit had a waist with a wide sailor collar, edged with ruffles, and a plaid bow tie—no wonder he liked it! Later on, he spent hours getting his hair brushed properly. He was ashamed of his sisters if they looked tousled or unkempt, as they usually did. Many years later, when he was in college, he refused to carry a Rhode Island Red rooster in a crate on the streets of Columbus, to oblige my father, who had sold it to another preacher.

Oscar was unlike Gerhard in every way. Gerhard loved books and was always the scholar. Oscar spent little time on his lessons and was always jolly and up to mischief. He was mechanically inclined and could make all sorts of things with his hands. Mama always said of Gerhard that he could not pound a nail in straight. Oscar was handier with tools than my father, and was always "the fixer" when things got out of order.

Miriam, the youngest, was pretty and much petted. She

was not shy, she had winning ways and attracted attention which she enjoyed. Although hers was a position of privilege, being the youngest and most dependent, she was not as spoiled as she might have been. She loved to wait on the four older ones and do everything they asked her to do. She was, in fact, their willing slave, and they made the most of it, often sending her on outrageous and impossible errands. Miriam was a great favorite of my father's. She could wrap Papa around her little finger and get everything she wanted. She had only one sorrow —her hair was as "straight as a poker" and she wanted curls.

Being the fourth child, I had three older ones to battle. So I was on the defensive most of the time. They loved to poke fun at me and tease me, Gerhard especially. They teased me because I refused to take castor oil. They teased me because I refused to accept the name *Maumee* as a proper name for a river. They teased me for everything under the sun. I had no peace, no rest. There was always something to be teased about. Why did they tease me so much? Perhaps, because I was vulnerable.

I suffered from intense shyness. My mother would say, "Now, Lois, don't be bashful!" Considering the many contacts with people in our home, I might have been bold. But I did not like to attract attention or to have people look at me. By contrast, Oscar was a great show-off, and Miriam was the friend of everybody. I preferred to hide behind my mother's long skirts, or to creep in behind the door where no one would think of looking for me.

While there were many advantages in being one of a large family, there were drawbacks, too. There was always strong competition among us, each had to battle for his own rights, but in so doing, we learned a ready give-and-take. Even as I fought for my own rights, I had to respect the other fellow's rights, too, and often give in to him, to admit that he was right and I was wrong.

Myself   I might have been a pretty little girl, but I did not have much chance. I had curly light blond hair, but wore it looped in tight braids and tied with ribbons, so my curls did not show. My eyes were blue, but turned green when I wore a green dress. At least, Gerhard said so, and teased me, calling them "cat eyes." I wore plain, severe, homemade dresses, with long sleeves and high necks, gingham, often horrible plaids, in summer, and wool in winter. My legs were always covered with long black stockings and my feet with high-topped shoes, buttoned with a buttonhook, except when we went barefoot in summer. Sunning was not popular, but sunbonnets were—all the little girls and women, too, wore them to keep the sun off. There was nothing about our garb to encourage vanity, and I am quite sure I never indulged in it.

We all had regular chores to do, and I don't know why mine was the most disagreeable one of all. For many years, it was my duty to take care of some ten or more lamps, filling them with kerosene—we called it "coal oil"—and how I hated it! The wicks had to be trimmed, smoky chimneys had to be washed, shined, and kept spotless, and this was a daily chore. I had to be careful not to spill the kerosene, and it was hard to get the smell of the oil off my hands, afterwards. We all had to carry water, bring in wood and coal, keeping woodboxes and coal buckets full. We helped with cooking, cleaning, washing, sewing, and whatever was going on. We got used to work at an early age, and never learned to evade it.

I remember my first day of school, at Anna, shortly after we moved there. I remember it because Papa gave me a new pencil box, filled with beautiful pencils. It was pretty with a sliding top that had a picture of flowers on it. I kept it for many years.

We had a piano in Anna and several of us took lessons from Anna Albers, a music teacher who came up from Sidney. Although I loved the singing at school, my interest in the piano was never stimulated. I took lessons for about two years, then, because I was "stubborn" and would not practice regularly, they were given up, much to my later regret. (At the age of twenty-seven, I tried to rectify this deficiency by taking lessons one summer. I learned only enough to play occasionally, for my own pleasure.)

While I was growing up, I had no spending money except what my father gave me, a nickel or a dime at a time. Children were not paid by parents for doing work around the home nor did they get a weekly allowance. Actually I had little need for spending money, as there was practically nothing I wanted; nothing I could do with it. Later on, in college, my father gave me my carfare. He wanted me to save what I was earning in the summers.

When I was eight, I had a serious illness, pneumonia, and again my life was despaired of. A cot was placed for me in the parlor, beneath the mantel, on which stood the eight-day marble clock, which chimed the hour and the half-hour. Little round pillboxes containing my pills were also kept on this mantel. The parlor became a sickroom, with the doctor coming and going. Anxious days and nights passed with my parents greatly worried. At last the crisis was passed.

There came a day when I was well enough to be carried to an armchair by an open window. There I had a miraculous vision. I looked out and saw the whole sky filled with apple blossoms, pink and white blooms of ethereal beauty against the deep blue of the sky! Like a vision of Heaven it struck me. So much beauty was more than I could bear. They found me crying and I had to be carried back to bed. It had been winter when I was taken ill. During the long weeks that I lay in bed, spring had crept up and given me a surprise. No spring since then has ever been more poignant or more beautiful.

Always, after this illness, my mother feared I would be the victim of "lung trouble." Again I acquired a halo! I became a heroine, and my brothers and sisters my devoted slaves. But it did not last long—I was soon put back in my proper place again.

I had an exaggerated moral sense as a child.

Once, at Finkenbine's store a real drama took place. I had been sent there on an errand, and while I was waiting, on impulse, I reached into a basket of English walnuts, picked one up and swiftly put it in my pocket. Glancing up, I saw the sharp eyes of Miss H——, the milliner, in the adjoining room, upon me, and heard her calling: "Here! Here! What are you doing?" I did not wait. Out of the store I ran, across the street and on toward home, fleeing down the back alley. When I was about halfway home, I threw the nut over somebody's chicken-yard fence. I did not want it anymore.

But that was not the end. On Monday evening, Miss H—— and her friend, who was my Sunday School teacher, came to the parsonage to call. I was terrified and tried to hide. I had never liked the milliner's cold hard eyes and her unfriendly manner. I knew she had come "to tell on me." When my mother called me, I went into the room in fear and trembling. I shook hands with the two ladies, expecting the worst. Miss H—— stared at me, but said nothing. The women began to talk. Papa pulled out his watch and said, "Time for bed," so I escaped.

I went to bed but could not sleep. My conscience troubled me. I waited a long time, long enough for the guests to make their departure. Then I crept down the stairs. I wanted to see my mother and to tell her of my misdeed. At the sitting-room door, I heard voices. They had not gone, after all. I stood and listened. It was my Sunday School teacher and she said: "Why didn't you tell me before yesterday? I would have asked her to confess in Sunday School!" She and Miss H—— laughed heartlessly.

I crept through the black hall and up the winding stairs and crawled into bed. I cried myself to sleep, for I knew now that my parents knew I was a thief. But from that day to this, neither my father nor my mother said one word about it, so perhaps they understood.

The winters of my childhood were real ones. With only heat from stoves, the floors of our house were cold and for years I suffered from chilblains. We used to apply thinly-sliced potatoes, but that did not help much. Whenever we went out, Miriam and I wore heavy coats, leggings that buttoned up with many buttons, and overshoes. On our heads we wore long, knitted stocking caps with tassels on the end. They could be pulled down to keep our ears warm. Of course, under all this was our heavy knitted underwear with long arms and legs; and various petticoats, some of flannelette, some of cotton with embroidery trim, tucks, and ruffles.

We five children had two sleds. The boys' sled was a low flat "belly-whopper"; the girls' was more elegant and stood higher. We took turns using them. One of my most poignant memories is of the time when I lost mine. There were few hills for coasting, so it was our habit to hitch the sled rope to the back of horse-drawn vehicles to get free rides.

Once I hitched to the back of a large bobsled, drawn by a lively team of horses. The farmer whipped up his horses to make them go fast. I fell off the sled, letting go of the rope, expecting the sled to slip loose. But the rope caught and held the sled and it went careening off into the country without me. I stood in the middle of the road watching it, tears rolling down my cheeks. I was sure that the farmer wanted my sled and meant to keep it. I would never see it again. It was hard to go home and report the loss of the sled and get a scolding for being so carelesss. I didn't even know the name of the farmer or where he lived!

But there was a happy ending. A few days later, Ruth Ailes, an older girl, brought the sled back to us. She had hitched out to this same farm, found the sled and recognized it as mine. I can never forget that sled! On the center panel was painted a bright red rose!

I was fortunate to have a younger sister to share my every moment and thought and activity. Miriam and I were constant companions. We did everything together—we slept together, dressed together, played together. We were never parted day or night. We never quarreled, we loved each other dearly. Our gingham dresses that Mama made, our long black stockings and high shoes were identical. For Sundays, we wore hats that were real hats, with crowns and brims and fancy trimmings, and elastics under the chins so that the wind could not blow them away.

We played together, but there was a difference in our play. Miriam's play was active, mine was passive. Miriam enacted drama with her dolls, while I, busy sewing for mine, watched her and Ethel Price in their play. I was on the sidelines, always the observer. Miriam and Ethel would make up plays for their dolls, making them talk and cry and sing and perform. Miriam was always the preacher at our funeral performances. I did not do these things. I watched and listened. I was the audience. From an early age, I wondered what other people were thinking and why they did what they did.

I began to sew for my dolls when I was six. Mama showed me how to cut a pattern, set in sleeves, how to gather a skirt to put it in a belt, how to make buttonholes, how to do hemstitching. She said, "If you are going to learn to sew, you might as well do it the right way." The box of scraps from her own dressmaking was my treasure box.

I decided I wanted to be a dressmaker when I grew up. I suppose my mother's interest in fine clothes was partly responsible. Sewing was creative, and it involved work with the hands, so it absorbed me. Each time Esther returned from Springfield, while she was in high school there, she was amazed at all the things I had made and at the "ideas" I had, ideas that never occurred to her at all.

I invented a workbasket, to be made of pieces of cardboard covered with cloth and fitted together, then tied with ribbon bows at the corners. "Aunt Janet" had a children's page each month in the *Woman's Home Companion,* which I always read avidly. I sent directions and diagram for the workbasket to her, and it was printed. Once I sent in a doll's nightgown that I had made, with lacy yoke and hemstitched hem. As an award for this, I received a piece of dress material and a doll's dress pattern, together with a note of praise from "Aunt Janet." I learned crocheting, tatting, and embroidery. Girls of my age were all doing these things at this period.

My love of gardening was instilled early. By the time I was eight, my mother and I studied the seed catalogs in the spring, made out orders for vegetable and flower seeds and gloated when they came. We both loved to watch a plant through its whole cycle of growth, from seed to bloom to seed again. We planted a vegetable garden, but our chief interest was in flowers. All summer we ate out of the garden and canned the surplus. The blooms on our beds of annuals and perennials were our pride and joy. While Esther and Miriam did the housework inside, Mama and I worked outside, busy with spade, rake, and hoe.

We visited greenhouses, too, making special trips to Sidney for the purpose. My mother indulged herself in exotic specimens—fuchsias, heliotrope, Jerusalem cherry, and choice begonias. She always had her beds of pansies, sweet peas, and roses. I shared all these creative interests with her. There was plenty of hard work to achieve results, but we did not mind. Weeding was endless, and there was plenty of hoeing to be done in the vegetable rows. We children had to pick off potato bugs and drop them into cans of kerosene. Grass and moss grew up between the red bricks in the sidewalks in the yard. We cleaned it out, on hands and knees, with a paring knife. It was not easy to grow house plants over winter in a stove-heated house. We often had to place thick newspapers inside the window panes to keep the cold out. But my mother's bay window full of plants was always a beautiful sight. I early learned that the gardener's life, like the farmer's, is governed by the thermometer, and he has to make many compromises with Mother Nature.

Once my father grew a grapefruit tree in a pot, as a house plant. I remember it well. It grew to a height of about three feet, it blossomed and bore a single fruit. First it was the size of a lemon, then it grew larger, as large as an orange. Then still larger! We all watched it in fascination. Six inches in diameter—would it never stop? At last the day came to cut it off and eat it. We had never seen or tasted a grapefruit before. We all stood and watched. My father cut it in slices and we each had a taste. Phew! Bitter! Nobody liked it! What an anticlimax!

This passion for flowers and gardening, inculcated when a child, has stayed with me all my life. It has been truly a creative outlet. In later years it expressed itself in a large rock garden in Connecticut and a tropical lath-house in Florida. All good things come from the earth, and to the earth we must go for refreshment and renewal of spirit.

Groping Towards Art My interst in art began in the third grade. My teacher, Rose Foster of Sidney, somehow found out that I liked to draw. Under her direction at the Anna school, I traced pictures of pretty flowers from seed catalogs, and painted them with watercolors. I had only a twenty-five-cent four-color box of Prang paints until 1907, when the fresco artist for the new church then being built, came from Lima, Ohio, to stay with us. He told my father, "This child has talent. She needs a better box of paints." So my father gave him three dollars and with it he bought me a Windsor Newton watercolor box at Lima. It had twenty or so colors and he said it would last a lifetime. It nearly did, being replaced only once.

With it, I began to be more ambitious. Under the fresco artist's direction, I copied covers of the *Woman's Home Companion,* and sent them in to "Aunt Janet," for the children's page. In 1907, when I was fourteen, I sent in a copy of a previous cover design, mother and baby, and received a post-card saying:

"Dear Lois:
    Your charming painting has won the $3.00 prize. A check will be sent you in a week or ten days. Lovingly,
                                                          Aunt Janet"

How well I remember my father putting his arm around my mother's shoulder and saying: "Just think! *Our* Lois has won the three-dollar prize!" It was a big moment for me. I have no memory of the arrival of the check or what I did with the three dollars—a huge amount to me at that time. Later, a copy that I made of another cover with a yawning baby was reproduced on Aunt Janet's page.

I began to enter my paintings in the Shelby County Fair at Sidney each fall, and won prizes there too. But my father shook his head, saying: "They would be good, if they were only original!" He had had experience in drawing himself as a young man, but he did not know how to tell me to be original. Nor did anyone else. Once I went out in the cornfield back of our house and tried to paint a row of corn-shocks, but the subject was difficult and my result was a failure. What a pity that no one told me to just draw all the things around me, to draw everything that I saw, instead of copying other pictures. I had no idea "how to be original" and it was many years before I learned. All the pictures I drew or painted before I was fifteen were copies. I did not begin the study of art until I went to college.

Except for sewing and gardening and copying pictures, I had no creative outlets as a child. My mother had a love of the beautiful and a desire to express it. I have a small plaque with a spray of delicate woodbine on it, that she painted as a young woman. My father, as I have told, made drawings for a few years. At one time, he became a member of the "Art Collectors Club" of Philadelphia and received at intervals reproductions of famous paintings, some of which he framed and hung on our walls.

All through my childhood and youth I was groping towards art, but I was badly restrained in self-expression. I had no art instruction in high school and a limited amount, mostly design, in college. So my real training did not begin until after I was twenty-two. I had to work a long time to overcome the restraints of earlier years, striving to achieve a degree of freedom in expression, never fully accomplished.

My background had given me no art. I never saw a real painting until I was eighteen. Little music—I never heard a concert or a symphony until after I was eighteen. How, out of such an atmosphere, can an artist grow? I followed only the vague gropings of instinct. Perhaps there was hidden away an inheritance from my ancestors. But in spite of the restrictions of my childhood, it was a good and wholesome background, implanting a love of people as well as of plants and growing things, and somehow in this perhaps unpromising soil, a seed was sown and nourished, the seed of creative life.

School   The old schoolhouse that I knew stood on a hill on the back street of Anna. Most of us who were young there were eager for learning. We loved its scuffed hallway, its whittled desks, its pot-bellied stoves, its dusty blackboards, and the soft erasers to be cleaned by slapping two together at an open window.

We used the Baldwin Readers—McGuffey was out of style in the early 1900's—and each year I read the new reader through in a day or two, then suffered boredom through the remainder of the year as the rest of the class plodded through it, page by page. We became good spellers, we had spelling matches every Friday afternoon, the best speller standing at the head of the line and the poorest at the foot. It was a sad event when the head missed a word and had to go to the foot, but it was not long until she caught up again. We were good at ciphering, too, and competed in exciting ciphering matches against each other. We learned penmanship as an art, and wrote beautifully. I marvel now at the thoroughness of our education in all these lines.

We had a fine music teacher, Frank Gephart, with an infectious personality. He came once a week and spent a part of the day in each of the four rooms. We had songbooks and he assigned songs to be learned. He carried a "pitch-pipe" in his pocket and used it to give us the pitch. We sang the notes: *do re mi fa sol la ti do.* He not only taught us to sing and to love singing, but to read notes, for which I have been ever grateful.

The school building had two floors, with center halls. There were two large rooms below, running from front to back, and two rooms above, with three grades in each room. Miss Lelia Fitzgerald was my first teacher and Miss Rose Foster my second.

There was a well with an iron pump in front of the school, where the children would line up for drinks from a common tin cup hanging on a chain. In winter we brought our sleds to school and coasted down the schoolyard hill to a hollow below. On this slope was the big boys' baseball field with a backstop. I remember it well, for once when I was coasting down, I hit the frame, slid under a brace and hurt my neck— a painful experience.

In a house beside the schoolyard lived a woman called Aunt Lyddy Nolan, who smoked a pipe. If a baseball ever landed inside her fence, she kept it and no amount of coaxing could induce her to give it back. All the schoolchildren hated her cordially.

On the back street, right beside the school, there was a "haunted house"—so the other children said. It had stood empty for a long time and boys with vivid imaginations reported seeing ghosts and hearing strange sounds inside at night. Clint Copeland, a Negro boy, told us about it. He lived across the street and carried water from the school pump for his mother. Once he went to get a bucket of water at nine o'clock at night. The ghost came out of the haunted house, came behind him, sneaked up, and grabbed him. He was so scared, he couldn't go back to get the bucket till daylight the next morning. After his fright wore off, he began to suspect that several boys had played "ghost," Gerhard Lenski among them.

But we girls stayed scared. I think we nourished our fright. We were sure we saw ghostlike faces and hands at the bleak black broken windows. We imagined we heard ghostlike cryings and wailings as the wind rattled through. We never walked past the house alone, and even when there were two or three of us with locked arms, we always let go and ran.

We ran home fast, too, for lunch each day, and after school because we were sometimes chased. From all our fears, there was always safety in flight.

We swallowed our dinner quickly and rushed back to school to get in line to play baseball. The boys had a team of their own. In the long summer evenings, after supper, we played tag, prisoners' base, hide-and-seek, and Blanchy-lie-low, our voices calling to each other through the evening stillness. We girls loved to play Statue, whirling each other into impossible poses, which we had to keep without toppling over. We never had any accidents. How we escaped broken arms and legs my mother could never understand.

I loved school and everything we did at school. I was always docile and obedient to authority. I am afraid I was a perennial "teacher's pet," but I hope I was not a prig. I was by nature shy and modest, never a braggart or an extrovert. Whenever we had Parents' Day, my teachers told my parents how much they enjoyed teaching me. I was always at the "head of the class" where my parents expected me to be. I was fortunate to grow up in an atmosphere of praise.

Esther and Gerhard had been sent to Springfield to stay with Aunt Willie and go to high school there. My first year in the Anna High School proved unsatisfactory. The teacher was belligerent and difficult and neither Oscar nor I learned anything from him. So in September, 1908, my parents transferred us to Sidney High School.

By today's standards, I suppose the Anna school of the early 1900's would be considered outmoded. But in looking back, I find that I got a solid basic training in the three R's, which has stood me in good stead all my life. I acquired a love of books and reading, a love of poetry and music, a curiosity about learning, and a keen desire for further education. What more could anyone ask?

Special Events Although Anna was a small town and not unusual or remarkable in any way, there were special events that gave real spice to life. There were Donation Parties for the preacher's family, Fourth of July and Christmas celebrations, summer thrashings on the farms, and most important of all, the coming of the first automobile in town, a portent of more radical changes to follow over the years.

Every once in a while there would be a Donation Party for the Lutheran preacher. This came at uncertain intervals, at no predicted time, and was always a surprise—to the family. Suddenly on a quiet summer evening, when we would be sitting on the front porch, watching the fireflies flitting through the dusk, after we children had come back, breathless and panting from a few lively games of Blanchy-lie-low, we would look up and see a long procession of solemn, silent people, walking in twos and threes, coming up the sidewalk from the church corner toward our house, with packages and bundles in their arms.

"A donation!" my mother exclaimed. "Goodness gracious! It looks like a donation!"

Mama was horrified at being caught in her old clothes, so we all ran. The girls' hair was not combed, the boys' faces were dirty, she herself had her oldest checked gingham apron on—how she hated surprises! But she always rallied and met the situation with poise and grace. My mother was not easily flustered.

Secret word had been passed around and the whole congregation came, loaded down with gifts—eggs, chickens, hams, sides of bacon, jars of fruit, jelly and jam, fresh fruit and vegetables, even house furnishings like towels and pillow cases. The people spent the evening and made a party out of it. Suddenly the whole house was filled with bright lights and loud talk and laughter. As if by magic, refreshments appeared on the table and my father's lighted Japanese lanterns flickered in the breeze out under the trees. The donation, being more or less an annual custom, was one way of supplementing my father's meager salary of seven hundred dollars a year.

We received gifts through the year, too, usually on Saturdays when the country people came to town. Whatever they had in abundance they shared with their pastor and his family. They brought us delicious homemade sausage, crocks of apple butter, hard, stiff and black, which had to be thinned down and softened before it could be used, bushels of apples and other fruits in season, root vegetables, squashes, pumpkins and potatoes, as well as butter, cheese, and poultry. Always at Eastertime we received dozens and dozens of eggs—the hens were laying well. The farmers' surplus kept our cellar filled around the year. At Christmastime, different church organizations would give the preacher "a present." That was how we acquired such a strange assortment of rocking chairs and fancy lamps and framed chromos for our walls. They were given by Confirmation classes, church choir, Young People's Society, or the Ladies' Aid Society.

"Another awful chair!" Mama would groan—privately, of course.

We took most of the awful rockers along when we moved to Columbus and always had them until the home was broken up. We were never able to get rid of them, and they were so substantial they never wore out. They became a part of our lives and a constant reminder of the good, loyal people from whom they came.

The Fourth of July was always a great occasion. All day long the Fogt Family Reunion was being held at Fogt's grove, a mile south of town. There were speeches, band music, and refreshments. Then in the evening everybody came to our house for my father's sensational display of fireworks. Preparations began early in the morning with the making of special shoots and stands. We children were busy, too, shooting off firecrackers and popping torpedoes. It was all as noisy and nervewracking as possible. Then the suspense—until it finally became dark enough!

Our front yard and the whole street filled up with people. They sat in rows on our lawn, they perched on our picket fence, boys climbed trees and telephone poles, and old ladies crowded neighboring porches. Suddenly my father appeared on the little second-story porch over the bay window of our house, which made a perfect stage for his performance. The firing of each skyrocket, Roman candle, and pinwheel was met with shouts of surprise and wonder from the excited audience, many of whom had never seen the like before. Sometimes three or four fireworks were shot off in unison—marvelous! A real fireworks display was unusual. My father was a great innovator in the town.

We, the preacher's family, visited many farms by special invitation, often going home with a certain family after church to stay for Sunday dinner. But the farm I remember best was Fred Ludwig's, a mile north of town. Summer thrashing at Ludwig's was a big event, which we would not have missed for anything. The children of half-a-dozen families were invited. The five Lenski children always went and spent the day. I suppose our parents went, too, although I do not remember that they were there. We five were the same ages as the five Ludwig girls—Mayme, Bertha, Nora, Margie, and Luella. Various boys came out from town to watch and act as water boys. A photograph taken by my father shows fifteen children, five boys and ten girls, the girls all wearing frilly sunbonnets except two with elaborately trimmed Sunday hats, sitting on bags of grain on the big farm wagon, ready to be hauled to town to the grain elevator.

I remember the thrashing machine puffing away and the wheat coming out to fill the bags, with the straw blowing out of the long stack at the other end. We must have often been in the way of the men working there, but they never complained or let us know it. Thrashing was something for children to enjoy. The best part of the day was the wonderful food, prepared by the women in the "summer kitchen" behind the farmhouse. The men ate at the first table and the women and children last. The huge white linen-covered table was filled with dishes of every imaginable kind of food, all kinds of meats, vegetables, pickles and sweet-sours, as well as desserts. There was always more than enough for everybody. I remember eating slices of homemade bread, spread with fresh country butter and Mrs. Ludwig's delicious cherry preserves that dripped all over my fingers—between the regular meals. Mrs. Ludwig made the best pot-pie and could cut the finest noodles in the county. And Margie was my best friend.

The father of another friend, Marie Fridley, was the first man in town to get an automobile, a small bright red two-seater, and it caused a sensation. After the novelty wore off, we children were given our first ride, and how exciting it was! But everyone, particularly our mother, distrusted the "machines" as they were first called. I thought it very strange when I first heard people speak of *driving a car*. We always drove a *horse,* how could you *drive* without a horse? You should speak of *running* or *operating* a machine, not *driving* it. The word *car* was wrong, too. A *car* was a passenger car or a freight car on the railroad, pulled by an engine. A *car* had to have tracks to run on. It was not this strange contraption, a horseless buggy, that ran of itself! My letters show that for many years our family continued to call the automobile "the machine."

I first heard the news of the assassination of President McKinley in Buffalo in 1901, when I was hitching up our horse, Pet, to our buggy. My father came down the alley with the *Cincinnati Times-Star* in his hand and read the news aloud. We children stood and gasped. I let the reins fall from my hands. Only the week before, my parents had returned from a trip to the Buffalo Exposition, while a neighbor stayed to keep house for us children. They had passed by the very spot where the assassination took place. My father was greatly moved by the sad news. I ran in the house to tell Mama and she cried. (A fictionized account of this incident is given in *A Little Girl of 1900.*)

Our Christmases   Our Christmases were sheer magic. They followed an exact ritual from year to year. The excitement began early in December, when our parents made a mysterious trip to Sidney and would not take any of us along. After their return, we obligingly pretended not to notice the bundles and packages which they smuggled indoors after dark and hid so carefully.

We began making presents ourselves. I can see yet the hemstitched handkerchiefs, the stuffed pincushions, the felt needle-books, and the embroidered pillow-tops I worked on so laboriously. For Papa I made calendars and pen-wipers. In those days he wrote with an ivory-handled pen, which had to be dipped into a bottle of ink, and wiped. At Sunday School we were given "pieces" to speak, and we studied hard to memorize them.

Days passed slowly—would Christmas never come? The first snow fell and that meant Christmas was getting nearer. At last, suddenly it was the day before Christmas and all our suspense seemed to crystallize. We could hardly contain ourselves. Mama and Esther were busy cooking and baking and the kitchen was full of delicious smells. A farmer brought a big Christmas tree, and the wife of another a large dressed turkey. On Christmas Eve, the children's service was held and we all went. Miriam and I, and often the boys, too, were on the program and had to speak our "pieces." I trembled from head to foot before my turn came, and then it was quickly over. Miriam, who could shout as loud as anyone at home, always spoke hers in a whisper, Mama said afterward.

A huge Christmas tree, lighted with candles which made it a thing of great beauty, stood at the front of the chancel in the church, and at its base were presents for all. Several men with long poles upon which were damp sponges kept walking around the tree, to put out candles as they burned down, to keep the tree from catching on fire. After the program was over, the children marched up by classes and gifts were passed out. Each child was given an orange, a box of hard candy, and a book. Oranges were real treats, as we so seldom had them, and we liked the hard candy, but we had our reservations about the books. They were too preachy. They had dull titles, like *Leroy, a Story for Our Boys; Naomi, a Story for Our Girls; From Darkness to Light; and From Poverty to Riches.*

Then home again, with excitement mounting until it was almost unbearable. We had no fireplace for hanging up our stockings, so we settled on chairs for our gifts. Each of us chose a chair before we were shooed off to bed. Miriam and I decided to remove only our shoes and our dresses, so it would not take long to get up in the morning. We kept on whispering and giggling, until Papa called to us to be quiet. How hard it was to settle down and sleep! And what a restless night, sleeping in underwear, petticoats, and stockings! We knew that mysterious things were happening downstairs. For days beforehand, the door to the front parlor had been kept tightly closed and locked, while strange noises could be heard inside. The keyhole revealed nothing.

Then came the magic words, "Get up! It's Christmas!"

Oscar was shaking us, and the boys were already up. Instantly out of bed, with our dresses over our arms, shivering from cold, all five of us crept down the creaking, winding stairs like noiseless mice. Halfway down, we were halted by the stern voice of Papa from the downstairs bedroom: "Back to bed! It's only three o'clock! Back to bed, all of you!" And a soft entreaty from Mama: "Can't you children sleep a little longer?"

Back we went and waited what seemed ages. Unable to sleep, we started down half an hour later, only to be sent back the second time. Finally, either the time passed or Papa gave up and we were allowed to stay. Papa came out, lit the big lamp and shook the ashes down in the base-burner, pouring more coal in at the top. It was still dark—the middle of the night to us—and this made the proceedings all the more mysterious.

We flew to our chairs. "Mine! Mine! See what I've got!"

There were never many gifts, but they seemed wonderful. Mittens and hair-ribbons or other articles of clothing, toy blocks or a wagon, a new head for my old doll whom I had named Beatrice because I thought the name so beautiful. Once Miriam got a doll's bed and I a doll's trunk (which I still have). Another year Miriam wanted "a real gold ring" because Ethel Price had one, and her cup of joy was full when she got it. I cannot remember wanting a gold ring myself, or receiving one, but I find I still have a little girl's ring, in a ring box in the doll trunk, which has stayed with me through the years. Miriam and I were usually treated exactly alike, so I probably got the ring at the same time she got hers. None of us were given toys such as children receive today.

But all these things were minor. The important thing was *books*. We each had a pile and could hardly wait to start reading them. Certainly Esther, the bookworm, could not. By breakfast time, she was halfway through one of hers, and bragging loudly, "It's the best book I ever read! The very best!" Books were our great joy and we were all soon flat on our stomachs on the floor or huddled in a bunch on the sofa, turning the pages over to see what delights the new book held. We all calmed down and after a time, managed to get dressed by the stove. Then our parents joined us.

The double doors to the parlor were opened, and there in all its glory stood our Christmas tree, with its lighted candles sparkling in the darkness, and a beautiful angel on top. Under the tree was the manger scene, a wooden stable beside a pond made from a mirror. Beside the stable were dolls dressed as Mary and Joseph, and a tiny baby doll in the manger. The stable roof and the fenced-in yard were covered with cotton snow. We loved the cotton lambs that kept falling over, the crooked cow and the donkey that had only three legs. It

66

would not have been Christmas without the Nativity scene. We had it through all the years of our childhood. We stood together beside the tree and sang *Silent Night*. Then we spoke our pieces.

Soon it was time for breakfast, a special one with Mama's fancy rolls, braided and twisted, with white icing on top, and fried country sausage, the best in the world. To our amazement, morning had come and the sun was shining! And look at the sideboard. Candy! One dish with chocolate peanut clusters and another with coconut bonbons and stuffed dates! Not to mention a big bowl of nuts and oranges. Was there no end to the wonders of Christmas?

Then the church bell was ringing again and it was time for church. We had to get ready for the Christmas morning service, and very reluctantly leave our treasures. Somehow we managed to sit through it, then home again. Home again, to a big turkey dinner and to all the joys of Christmas. And then at last, it was over, except for one thing, the books. They lasted through the year, not one year, but many.

In 1965, my brother Gerhard wrote me:

> "How wonderful those early Christmases were! I think they gave to you, as they did to me, a lasting love of books."

Books were always a part of our lives. We loved them, revered them and preferred them to all other gifts. Other things happened on Christmas Day—the service at church, the big Christmas dinner, visits from friends and neighbors, but all these fade away. The memory of good books remains.

We all loved to read, but judging from her reputation, Esther must have eclipsed us all. Even back in Springfield days, she had been known as "a terrible reader" and bribed Gerhard to hook up her high-button shoes for her, by reading *Robinson Crusoe* aloud to him. She often escaped dishwashing by "having her nose in a book." Miriam and I followed Esther's bad example. All through our childhood, we all read every book we could get our hands on, and there were never enough. I have often wondered where the books we had in our home came from. There were no bookshops in the small towns near us, Springfield and Columbus were far away in horse-and-buggy days, so I can only conclude that my father ordered them from publishers' catalogs. Some were gifts from friends in Springfield.

These are the books I grew up on:

Little Women, Jo's Boys, etc. by Louisa May Alcott

> We loved and read all her books over and over again.

The Wide, Wide World by Susan Warner

Elsie Dinsmore by Martha Finley

> I must confess I loved and wept over both these books.

The Five Little Peppers and How They Grew by Margaret Sidney

The Little Lame Prince by Miss Muloch

Poems by Eugene Field

Child Rhymes by James Whitcomb Riley

> We learned and recited many of these poems.

The Birds' Christmas Carol, Polly Oliver's Problem, Rebecca of Sunnybrook Farm by Kate Douglas Wiggin

> Next to Louisa Alcott, Kate Douglas Wiggin was my favorite author. All her books were read over and over, and were dearly loved.

Mrs. Wiggs of the Cabbage Patch by Alice H. Rice

> This and *The Birds' Christmas Carol* made a special appeal to me due to their humor and pathos.

The Wonder Book by Nathaniel Hawthorne

Little Lord Fauntleroy by Frances Hodgson Burnett

> A great favorite, sentiment and all.

Black Beauty by Anna Sewell

> We loved horses because Mama did.

Helen's Babies by John Hibberton

The following were general family books, owned mostly by Esther and the boys, but read by us all:

Robinson Crusoe; Swiss Family Robinson; Arabian Nights; Baron Munchausen; Prose Tales by Edgar Allan Poe; *Uncle*

Tom's Cabin; Pilgrim's Progress. The boys had many of the Henty and Alger books, but I never read any of them.

Other books that we did not own, but may have borrowed from the Sidney Public Library were: *Gulliver's Travels,* Grimms' and Andersen's *Fairy Tales, Red, Blue,* and *Green Fairy Tales; Hans Brinker and the Silver Skates.* We were awarded certain books as premiums by the Shelby County Fair, for schoolwork exhibited there. They were mostly *Eclectic School Readings.* I do not recall that we had any sort of library at the Anna school, or any "storybooks" to read there.

I grew up without benefit of *Alice in Wonderland, Treasure Island,* and *Huckleberry Finn.* There may have been others that I missed as well, but our diet in books was a good one, considering how few books there were for children to read then, compared with the vast riches of children's literature today.

In the years from 1884 to 1895, my father subscribed to *Harper's, Century,* and *Scribner's* magazines, and also to the *Atlantic Monthly.* He valued them so highly that he bound them into large volumes on his own binding press. They stood for years on the shelves of his bookcases and were a constant source of literary enjoyment. They contained stories by Oliver Goldsmith, Charles Dudley Warner, Sara Orne Jewett, and many other fine writers. They were full of delightful illustrations by Charles Dana Gibson, Alice Barbour Stephens, Howard Pyle, F. D. Millet, Peter Newell and others. I inherited and prized these volumes, only recently parting with them, when I donated them to several university libraries, where they are greatly cherished.

My mother was a staunch subscriber to the *Woman's Home Companion,* which was to have a hand in shaping my artistic career. We children took the *Youths' Companion.* It was a true companion to all five of us for many years, as it had something for all ages. We fought over who would get to read it first. The "Children's Page" was for Miriam and me, while the boys and Esther had all the thrills of reading the adventure stories. We saved all the issues, for we could not bear to throw them away, and read them over and over again. Some of the newspapers were starting to print comics or "funnies" as we called them. I remember *Foxy Grandpa, Buster Brown,* and *Happy Hooligan.*

Tragedy   All small towns have their human tragedies, but few of them in Anna reached me. As a young child I knew that people died, for I often saw photographs taken by my father of babies or older people in their coffins. One day the H—— children's mother died. They told me about it and took me in their house to see her. I had often seen their mother at their back door and heard her calling them to come in. Now she lay there quietly, lips still, eyes closed, hands folded. I took one look and ran out, crying.

The H—— children turned to me, dry-eyed, and said: "What are *you* crying for? She's *our* mother!"

Somebody's house burned down, I cannot remember whose, but only the ghastly fact. It was always exciting to hear the *clang-clang-clang* of the fire bell, to see the volunteer firemen running to their places, and to watch the fire engine go roaring down the street. We always ran to see each fire, but most of them were not serious. This one was. The furniture stood about on the lawn, the roof fell in and everybody cried. The mother and children sat on a sofa, crying. I heard the little girl ask, "Where will we go now?"

It worried me for weeks. If your house burned down, where did you go to live? Out in the woods? At last I could bear it no longer. I asked my mother and she said the woman's brother had given the family a house to live in. They had moved to another town. I felt better.

I was an innocent among my girl friends. They hinted that they knew things I did not know. They told me that a certain child had no father. I did not believe it. Some time afterwards, I saw the church record book lying open on my father's desk, and the record of a baptism in it. It gave the mother's name, and then in my father's handwriting: "The mother says the father is ———." The name was not the same as the mother's. Each time I saw that small child, I knew she was somehow different.

On a farm where we visited one Sunday, we children played in the back yard, and in the field beyond, under some trees, there stood an old log cabin. I ran there to hide, and suddenly at the cabin window, behind iron bars, I saw a horrible distorted face appear, with hair flying in all directions. I heard horrible sounds coming out of a large red mouth. The farmer's children called me back, but I did not need to be called. Screaming and terrified, I could not run fast enough. I ran so fast I stumbled and fell, bruising my knee. They scolded me:

"Don't go there! Don't you ever go there again!" they cried.

I had seen enough, I never wanted to go again. But for days I wondered: Did *they* know? Did *they* know about that horrible old witch? I did not dare ask. Not till years later did I learn that this was a way of caring for mental patients in the home.

Once at school, when I was in the Third Room, upstairs, I happened to walk past an open window and look out and down. I saw a man running along the street, then another came running behind him and still another. I could not move, I stood and watched. At first I thought a house must be on fire, but I heard no fire bell ringing. I listened.

The first man shouted: *"Mr. F—— has hung himself! Mr. F—— has hung himself!"*

Then I realized that the teacher was calling me by name. I turned, and I could only repeat the words in a whisper: *"Mr. F—— has hung himself!"* All the children jumped up and ran to the window. More people were running now to the man's house on the back street. The teacher quieted us down and tried to get our attention back on our lessons.

There was a further sequel. The moment school was dismissed, we children all ran, too, to gaze on the house of tragedy. To my amazement, I saw my own father standing inside the door, his arms around the stricken young daughter, trying to comfort her. It was one of the first intimations I had had of my father's role of spiritual advisor in the community, and I never forgot it. Details of the tragedy became active rumors and the little town buzzed.

So did sorrow enter the old school on the hill, and so did tragedy touch the lives of the children, many of them for the first time.

Sunday and Church   The church had a very important place in our lives. It governed and controlled all our thoughts and actions. Sunday was the most important day of the week. I well remember hearing Grosspapa Lenski say that he never did any tailoring on Sunday, because it would be a sin. Only the most necessary work was done on Sunday. It was a day to think of spiritual things and for visiting.

Saturday meant getting ready for Sunday, getting our bodies, our clothing, our food, our thoughts, and the house ready for Sunday. It was cleaning day. The house had to be thoroughly cleaned and the bare floors scrubbed, fresh sheets put on the beds, fresh table covers and linen laid out. Food had to be cooked, cakes and pies baked, and our Sunday clothing put in order.

Sunday began with the ringing of the church bell. The very tone of the church bell gave Sunday a special flavor. It felt different from all other days. We spoke in lower voices as we quietly put on our Sunday clothes. We girls had special Sunday dresses and the boys Sunday suits, we had Sunday hats and Sunday shoes, which were never worn on weekdays. Later, when they had lost their first bloom, or were replaced by something newer, they were demoted to "everyday" or "school" wear.

First we went to Sunday School, while Mama stayed at home and prepared Sunday dinner. Then she joined us at church. We *always* went, we never stayed at home or thought of skipping, so deeply ingrained was the habit. I am sure that if we had stayed at home deliberately, we would have been miserable. Constant attendance at Sunday School and church meant hearing and memorizing untold numbers of Bible verses and hymns, any one of which could be repeated or sung at a moment's notice. What an invaluable heritage this was for a child to have these beautiful words so imbedded in his consciousness that they would never leave him!

We children, even when very young, went to both Sunday morning and evening services, including those that were in German. My father preached in both languages and we listened, although we did not understand German. My father was a German scholar, his parents, although they were not German, spoke nothing else. No German was spoken in our home, at my mother's request. I do not know why she objected to it. Anna was a German community and we heard German spoken all around us. We even learned to understand certain phrases, and later, when I studied German in college, it was very easy for me. But we never tried to speak it. I have regretted this ever since.

In the old frame church, the women sat on one side of the center aisle and the men on the other, in old-world style. But my mother was a rebel. She loved to walk in, after the service had begun, holding Miriam and me by the hand, and boldly sit down on the men's side. I did not realize until many years later, how courageous she was in thus upsetting local custom. We sat demurely by her side, listening to the rustling of her silken skirts and to her beautiful voice as she sang the well-loved hymns. She was always the best-dressed woman in the congregation and her voice the loveliest.

And there was Papa in the pulpit, with his finger pointing at sinners in the congregation! He was a fearful and somewhat terrifying person, speaking in reverberating, ringing tones, with power in his delivery and magnetism in his voice. No wonder he was popular in the Synod, and as one of their finest preachers, traveled far and wide to preach all over Ohio and the northwest. Yes, there was Papa in the pulpit, dressed in his long black robe, relieved only by the white bands at his collar, which Mama had to wash and starch and iron so carefully. Papa, important, forbidding, sometimes fiercely angry and unapproachable, who later that same day back at home at the dinner table, became just plain Papa, beloved and friendly again. We looked up to him with genuine awe and respect, and at the same time, we loved him dearly. Each Sunday, when church was over and the women crowded around the preacher's wife, someone was sure to say, with a laugh: "Didn't *they* catch it today!"

The new church built in 1907 had a pipe organ, and my brother Oscar was given the job of pumping it, for which he was paid twenty-five cents an hour. A door in the side paneling of the chancel opened into a little back room behind the organ, with all its great pipes overhead. A heavy wooden arm protruded from the body of the organ, and Oscar had to pump this up and down. One evening he fell asleep, and when the organist started to play, there was no music. My father, gown and all, quickly stepped through the secret door in the paneling, woke the boy up, set him to work, and soon the organ was pealing again.

Sunday afternoons at home were spent in quiet play or reading books. Sometimes visitors came and sat on the upholstered chairs in the parlor. I had to go in and shake their hands, in terror, but Miriam was never afraid. She was littler than I, but she had more courage. In summer, Sunday callers often walked with Mama and Papa out in the garden, we children trailing along, to look at the blooming flowers or to admire the vegetable crop. On Sunday evening the church bell ran again, called its people to worship. We went again to church, Miriam and I falling asleep one on each side, leaning against Mama's arms. After the service was over, Papa took off his robe and came to help Mama pilot us home.

Funerals played an important part in my life, although I

was never taken to a real one. We always knew when somebody had died, because of the slow tolling of the church bell. It was a signal to us to start counting and keep on counting the number of years that the person had lived. The funeral procession usually passed in front of our house on its way to and from the church. The hearse was ornate, black with glass windows at sides and end, and four black tassels at the corners. There were black silk curtains draped inside, shielding the casket, and there were black waving plumes on the horses' heads. Sometimes, if a child died, a beautiful white hearse was used. Behind the hearse come a long line of surreys and buggies, which we called "rigs," bearing the mourners dressed in black, the women draped in deep mourning veils.

Miriam and I loved to watch the procession, peeking out between the long lace curtains at the bay window in the parlor, and counting the rigs. Mama was expected to go to the funeral, of course, so we were left alone. Ponto, our dog, did not like the tolling of the bell and would start to howl, so it was our task to keep him quiet.

The photographs which my father took of babies, children, and older people in their coffins, were, I suppose, a comfort to the survivors. We saw them frequently, while he was developing and printing them, and admired them very much. To us, there was nothing sad or morbid about them. Playing funeral with our dolls became a regular ritual. We put the dolls in shoeboxes, dug holes in the ground, buried them with a long sermon and a few hymns, and put flowers on the graves. It was not a morbid but a happy ritual, for we always dug them up again!

Being brought up in a parsonage had its advantages and some disadvantages. A parsonage is not like a quiet, private home. It is almost as public as a church or a school. People were always coming and going, all kinds of people. Very early we got used to that, and very early we learned to treat all people alike no matter who they were. We learned to be kind, polite, and considerate to all. At least we tried to be. . . .

Our doors were never locked, anyone could walk in at any time. When a knock came or the door opened, we never knew who it might be—a farmer with a gift of smoked ham, a troubled woman in need of advice, a passing tramp begging for a handout, a visiting preacher to spend the night (they came often); a student selling Bibles, a choir director to make a complaint, a lightning-rod salesman or an insurance agent; a bereaved family to arrange for a funeral or a bride and groom to be married. It was amazing, the number and variety of people who kept coming.

Our visitors were always "company." Some stayed and stayed, interrupting my mother in her regular work. Some my father took care of in his study, with the door shut tight. Some stayed over night, for this was a day of open hospitality, when everyone who came was asked to stay for the next meal or to spend the night. No one was ever turned away. The guest room was always ready and there were always clean sheets on the clothesline. Strangers we had never seen before often stayed for meals.

No matter who came, they were treated with respect. My parents looked for the good in people and usually found it. It was a wholesome atmosphere in which to grow up, for we saw our parents living their religion not on just one day of the week but on all seven. They never preached to us about our relations to other people. They loved and respected people of all kinds and had dedicated their lives to helping them. We children tried to follow in their footsteps. Attitudes deeply imbedded in heart and mind during childhood become a part of oneself. They can never let go, can never be shaken off. For this reason, I think, there has never been a barrier between plain people and myself, a barrier which many people do feel and which has to be broken down before they can understand them.

It was not easy for me to meet people when I was a child. When guests were there, we were always expected to come into the room and to shake hands. I cannot forget my suffering, as I stood behind a closed door, trying to summon up enough courage to do as I was told. It was such an easy thing —to open the door, go in, shake hands, and say, "How do you do?" But the more I hesitated, thinking about it, the harder it became. For years I suffered from intense shyness, and even now I often have acute attacks. To approach a closed door and go in still sends shivers down my spine.

Because our father was the Lutheran minister, everyone looked up to us. We children had to be more or less on our good behavior all the time. People expected us to be better than other children. We soon sensed that and tried to live up to it, although we often failed. Not that being good kept us from being happy—it didn't. My father was strict, he did not approve of dancing, card-playing, swearing, or taking the Lord's name in vain. We did not dance or play cards, but we took music lessons. We refrained from doing many things that other young people of our age were doing. We had to keep our own counsel, not talk too much, above all, not judge others. I learned to stand on the sidelines and be an observer. Of all the lessons I learned as a child, this is the most important, and has served to guide me all my life. Stand aside— look and listen. Do not sit in judgment on others. Try to see their good points and forgive their faults.

Because we had to treat all people alike, we made few or no intimate friends. No confidences could be given or received. We were the preacher's children, a special class, set apart. We did not do what other children did, we were looked up to, we had to set a good example. We grew tired of hearing these words. It was a hard role to play. It was not easy, even in our small intimate world, to be always in the public eye, knowing people would criticize us no matter what we did. But that we tried our best, I am certain.

Growing Up I had a passing acquaintance with Sidney, before I went to high school there. Old Pet, our horse, was the connecting link. Sometimes my mother would take two or three of us children in the phaeton and drive to Sidney on Saturday for shopping. It was eight miles up and down hill on a gravel road, so we always started early and made a day of it. I remember an ice-cream parlor, where we sometimes stopped, and Thiedick's Department Store, where my mother bought me a knitted brown jacket, which the clerk called a "sweater." We often went to my mother's dressmaker's shop on a second floor, for a "trying-on." Perhaps it was these visits which made me yearn to be a dressmaker.

Soon the Interurban Railway came to Anna, and this made the trip to Sidney shorter and easier. The street was dug up past our house by a bevy of men, posts were set, and tracks were laid. My father took photographs of all the workmen, and soon the huge noisy cars began clattering and banging past our house, rattling and shaking all our windows. At this time, Esther had left Wittenberg College in Springfield without graduating and was teaching at Four Mile School, so she too rode the Interurban. We had to catch the 6:50 A.M. trolley. It would pass our house, go a block or two and stop. One after the other, Esther, Oscar, and I would come flying out of the front door, putting on coats and hats as we ran. The first one to get on the trolley would beg the conductor to wait for the others. He was obliging and would not give the signal to start until we all got there. In Sidney, the cars stopped at one side of the Courthouse Square, and Oscar and I had to walk under a railroad and up a hill to the old Fourth Ward Building.

It was an important day for me when I started as a sophomore at Sidney High School. Everything was different. In Anna there had been only one teacher for all three grades— a man who chewed pills incessantly. Now I had a different teacher for each subject, and how I enjoyed my studies. I especially remember two English teachers, pretty Miss Louise Reddish, and dignified Miss Frances Sharp. In my English classes I did my first writing—essays, stories, and book reports.

In the early 1900's, to show that a girl was growing up, she put her hair up and her skirts down, and a boy put on his first pair of long trousers. At Sidney High, I wore my hair in a pompadour (Esther and the other young ladies wore "rats") with a stiff black bow at the back of my head. I had a wide box-pleated, green plaid wool skirt that fell to the floor on both sides of my seat and became very dusty. We wore shirtwaists with tucks in front, a tight collar around the neck, held either with a pretty breast pin or a lace jabot. Sometimes we wore middy blouses with sailor collars and a big bow in front.

High school brought me closer than ever to books, for now I had the use of a library. The Sidney Public Library was located on the second floor of Monumental Building, diagonally across from the courthouse. We had to go up a long flight of stairs. I must have had long waits for the Interurban, which I spent in the library. I was voracious and read all the books I could check out. I was greatly impressed with the neat block printing of my name on my library card, and for years I thought that librarians all had a special calligraphy of their own. Now my old favorites, Wiggin, Alcott, and Burnett were being replaced by new favorites—Dickens, Thackeray, and Scott. Dickens above all with his vivid word pictures of real people, their trials and temptations, their sorrows and their joys. I wept and laughed and exulted with Dickens. There was no end to a young reader's happiness.

By graduation time, I knew that we were soon to move to Columbus. My father was to return to Capital University, his Alma Mater, as professor of classical languages and theology, and was later to become Dean of the Theological Seminary. This meant a chance for me to go to college, which I would not otherwise have had. That summer, 1911, Frances Sharp, my Senior English teacher, wrote me a letter, saying:

"I hope you will specialize in English in college, for I feel sure you will do some form of creative work."

(It was twenty-five years later before I was able to send her a copy of my book *Phebe Fairchild, Her Book,* a work of which I was truly proud, and which I felt had fulfilled her prophecy.)

With our move to Columbus in 1911, I left my childhood behind me.

STUDENT DAYS

COLUMBUS AND COLLEGE 1911–1915

A New Life

(Letter)   Lancaster, Ohio
                                            August 1, 1911

"The folks at home are packing up and Miriam and I were shipped here to be out of the way. I am to go to Ohio State and have decided to take the course for High School teachers. Don't know yet what I will specialize in. I am getting scared already."

                                            August 14, 1911

"Miriam and I can hardly wait to get to Columbus, and see that *wonderful new house* and get it fixed up just scrumptious. We think no one can do it but us, especially our own room!"

We left our "parlor set" of furniture behind for our successor. Parlors were going out of style, and in the new house which the college had built for us on the campus, there was none. My father's crayon portrait and the easel disappeared, too. The only record I have of our move is a few letters, among them one from Aunt Ida, Uncle Ed's wife, then living in Lancaster. She wrote to me, saying:

"Dear Lois:

I am very glad you and Miriam are coming to stay until your goods arrive. As for Collie and the cat, I am willing to keep them, but you would have to buy a chain for Collie, as we have no shed dog-proof and our yard is all open. The cat I could shut down cellar, to keep her away from the parrot. . . ."

We were willing to leave furniture and my father's photographic plates behind, but not the dog and the cat. (Collie was Ponto's successor.) I did not like Aunt Ida's noisy parrot much, but did enjoy a little girl of three from next door who came over every day. She brought her doll and a few toys, settled herself at my feet, and talked. I sat with pad and pencil in hand and took down her conversation verbatim. She was unusually loquacious for her age. Why I took it down I do not know, as I had never done anything like this before. That fall in my class in freshman English, I handed in this document for a theme, I suppose, on an unspecified subject. To my astonishment and embarrassment, the professor read it aloud to the class and commended the author as a "perspicacious observer"!

My parents were happy to move to Columbus, not only because of their personal associations there, but because it meant a chance for a college education for the children. Although I lived only four years in Columbus, during college, it was the place of my beginnings in more ways than one. My mother was born there, my grandmother's home had always been there, my father and uncles were all educated there— and as it turned out later, my parents were to live there for the rest of their lives and finally to be buried there.

Columbus has always epitomized Ohio for me. There is

something about the looks of the streets and the stores, the landscape and the freshness of the air, the look on the faces, the flatness of the voices, the intonation of the words—the "uh-huh" and the "all-righty"—and above all, in the taste of the food—fried chicken, cole slaw, and apple pie—that is unlike any other part of the country and definitely spells OHIO. Whenever, after years of being away, I return to the Buckeye State, I recognize this Ohio feeling, and I feel I am going home.

Now, in 1911, my childhood was over. I was no longer a child but a grownup. I was eighteen, entering college.

Capital University was not co-educational in 1911, so I entered Ohio State. The cost of my college education must be one of the lowest on record, ten dollars tuition for each semester or twenty for the year, plus the cost of my books, all purchased secondhand at the College Book Store. I lived at home, and for this reason, was unable to participate in social activities at the college. My mother was not well, I had to help with cooking and housework and this meant staying up late at night to get my studying done. My father often came into my bedroom at midnight and turned out my light, telling me I had studied enough and it was time for bed. (Esther married and left home in 1912, and this put added home responsibility upon me.)

My college life consisted of long trolley rides from the east end of Columbus to the north end, transferring at High Street. The trolley stopped at every street corner for people to get on and off, so it took a full hour to reach my destination. I did a great deal of studying along the way. I had to spend long hours reading assignments in the college library and often got home very late. One of my instructors told me, years later, what a serious student I had been. Actually, there was no fun in my life at all at this time, and very little diversion.

My parents thought I should prepare for teaching. Teaching was still, as late as 1915, considered the most respectable profession for a woman, although there was a movement toward participation in other fields. So I entered the College of Education. I disregarded my high school English teacher's advice to specialize in English, for like most young people I felt I knew best. Instead, for my electives, I took all the art courses I had time for, venturing timidly into this unknown field, simply because I liked to draw. These were chiefly courses in design and lettering, the latter with Thomas E. French, an authority, in the College of Engineering. I also took a course in engineering drawing with him, so that later I was able to draw up house plans and specifications, complete enough for a contractor to build from. My mother and I had for many years enjoyed a practice of studying house plans in magazines. My lettering courses proved very useful later, too— I was able to hand-letter all my own book jackets and title pages. Only in my senior year was there any figure-drawing from the costumed model, so I made little progress in what I needed most.

In my senior year I had to do some weeks of practice teaching in art in the public school, under observation. My instructor gave me the following report:

> "The lesson was thoroughly enjoyed by the class. I noticed no lack of interest or careless work. The four boys near me never varied from the beginning to the end of the lesson in their enthusiastic efforts. This will not always happen—few lessons will make such a universal appeal to the interests of a class—but I felt that it was also due to the presentation of the lessons that had proceeded it and which had aroused their interest."

I found German easy, for although I had never tried to speak it, I had heard it constantly during my childhood, so for a time, I served as a "reader" in German for a blind girl. I carried my own lunch each day and my father gave me money for carfare. After I began earning, he insisted that I put the money into a savings account at the bank. The only thing I spent money for was books. As early as 1913, I began buying books for a library of my own. I used to haunt the bookshop opposite the capitol on High Street. There I bought Everyman's Classics, lovely small inexpensive volumes—Shakespeare, Cooper, Poe, and practically all of Dickens, of whom I was so fond. There is no doubt that this initial grounding in the novels of Dickens had a definite influence on the writing I was to do in the future. Other adult authors whose philosophy affected my later work were William James, Tolstoy, especially his accounts of his peasant school at Yásnaya Polyána, and Albert Schweitzer.

Playground Children While I was in college, I used to have a group of neighbor children come to my house every Saturday afternoon, so I could tell them stories. I was studying French and German, so I translated French and German folktales to have more stories to tell. I gave the children refreshments, too. Once I remember I made lemon Jello for them, but they would not eat it, they preferred ice cream, they said. They were not so fussy about the stories I told them. They listened to all—good, bad, and indifferent! They were a happy enthusiastic group and I loved every minute with them.

I happened upon a copy of Sara Cone Bryant's book, *How to Tell Stories to Children,* in the bookshop uptown, and found it full of help and inspiration. About this time also, I bought a copy of *The Golden Windows* by Laura E. Richards. I told these tales over and over again and loved them as much as the children did.

Our home was on Capital University campus. Following the example of other college boys who were always looking for odd jobs to do, my brother Gerhard began teaching recreation on one of the Columbus city playgrounds in his summers. Through him, I learned that college girls were also employed and I made application. It did not pay much, but it was an opportunity for me to be with children. During the winter months we playground teachers had to attend special training classes, carried on by the city's Department of Recreation.

At one of the city playgrounds, I was to teach crafts, which meant sewing and paper cutting. I was given instruction in these, with concrete suggestions as to projects to be carried out with the children. I went to the Columbus library and found books to help me with supplementary ideas, and this led me to a study of some of the ideas and methods of the early educators, Froebel, Pestalozzi, and Montessori. The crafts teacher was also expected to help the regular recreation teacher whenever possible, so the training included the learning of ring games, singing games, and folk-dancing. I found all this most enjoyable, as it was all new to my experience.

Photographs taken at Goodale Park in 1914 show me wearing a loose khaki-colored uniform with leather belt, long skirt to my ankles, and a floppy hat pushed down over the back of my head. One, with a group of unkempt girls, is labeled: *"The bunch that gave so much trouble but was really good at heart."* Another photo of little ones is labeled: *"My paper class,"* and a group of ten-year-olds: *"My sewing class, all good workers."*

At this time I happened to find the books of Myra Kelly, *Little Citizens, Little Aliens,* and others, published before 1910. Myra Kelly was born in Dublin, came to the United States as a child and became a teacher of young children in New York's East Side from 1890 on. I enjoyed her books very much, and my style of writing in the following notes is definitely influenced by hers.

I seem to have made a feeble attempt at keeping a diary, but only a few fragments still exist, labeled *Playground Episodes:*

"The children were all frantic with joy that first day, when you, the new sewing teacher, arrived. You were greeted with open arms and hearts, in a series of tight hand-clasps and hugs, which were the mere forerunners of all that affection which was to be heaped upon your unjust head before the summer was over. The genuine welcome warmed your heart, and you vowed then and there to love the children every one. You sat down for a while in the grass with them, waiting for the janitor to appear and unlock the building. You tried to fix the names of this first half-dozen or so in your mind, but the crowd began to swell, and you decided not to be so foolish.

"It took a long time that first day for you to take a good view of the whole situation and to prepare your fortifications and battlements against the incoming storm. The first necessary step was the terrible task of taking the census—the names, ages and addresses of that mob of little women. A large number of them did not know where they lived, or said it was 'across the street' or 'down the alley' or 'over that way somewhere' in some corner, some place unknown. Others did not know their ages, or when their birthdays were. Some had birthdays 'next year,' 'the day before *our* Easter' on 'the 29th of February' and various equally inaccessible dates.

"You stood abashed when a small girl admonished you: 'You make all the time mistakes. You shouldn't put no *h* on *Sara!*' "

The diary shows that I became very much attached to certain children, including some that were problems, but who responded to the appeal of the sewing and craft work that I taught them. These three summers on the Columbus playgrounds were delightful and taught me a great deal.

The Dayton Flood For the Easter vacation in 1913, I went to Phillipsburg, Ohio, near Dayton, to visit my sister Esther. She had married Rev. William Ferne, a Seminary graduate, the year before and he was serving his first pastorate in this small town. It was a rainy week—it rained and rained and rained. When it was time for me to return to Columbus, it was still raining hard, reports were heard of water in people's cellars and of roads being washed out. So I postponed my departure for a day. By this time, water was high in yards and cellars in town, no mail was coming through and traction cars and trains had stopped running. We began to hear wild reports of a terrible flood in Dayton and vicinity. There were no radios then and rumors were carried by word of mouth.

On Wednesday we hitched up the horse to the buggy and drove to Dayton, or tried to. We got into a long slow procession of buggies and automobiles crawling along in the pouring rain. Finally we reached the outskirts of the city. There we saw men in boats rowing down the middle of the street, and houses with water up to the second story. We went into a schoolhouse and saw tables piled high with all kinds of eatables, clothing and shoes, and other tables set to feed the rescued. A church nearby was used for the same purpose, as were all the schools and churches in Dayton. We learned that both the Stillwater and Miami rivers had flooded a wide area. Returning to Phillipsburg, it was freezing cold, despite a wool blanket pulled up to our chins in the open buggy. The next day we counted over a hundred conveyances going to Dayton with provisions, including a load of twenty-five caskets.

I was worried about the delay in getting back to school. Finally, at the end of the second week, I managed to get a special pass to cross the city of Dayton and take the train to Columbus. The water had gone down, the streets were filled with broken paving, broken plate-glass windows, mud-covered pianos, and other furniture, and with dead horses and dogs. It was a shocking sight which I never forgot. On the train, which was crowded with flood refugees, I listened to tales of horror and danger. I sat beside a woman who told me she had had nothing to feed her baby but cabbage for over a week. The child slept peacefully.

When we finally reached Columbus, our train stopped on the west side of town and did not go to the railway station at all. I was astonished to learn that the Scioto River was flooded, too, and the entire west side of Columbus had been under water, with many houses washed away. How I managed to get home to the east side, I do not remember. There, my family were greatly worried. They knew I was to have started home on the first day of the flood. They had tried to reach us by telephone and telegram at Phillipsburg without success. Gerhard was the one who reassured my parents: "Don't worry! Lois is able to take care of herself!"

I did not miss school after all. College had not reopened because of the flood, and students were asked to volunteer for flood relief. I worked several weeks in a schoolhouse on the west side, giving out clothing to flood victims. Here I came into direct contact with grief, suffering, and dire need for the first time, as I listened to the people's stories and tried to comfort them.

Graduation In my senior year I made the drawings for several campus publications, and because of these I was chosen Art Editor for the 1915 yearbook, the Makio. In this issue I made full-page cartoonlike drawings for the headings of the different sections. This was my first work for reproduction.

In June, 1915, four degrees were awarded to the Lenski family on a single day. I received the degree of Bachelor of Science in Education, Oscar received his Bachelor of Architecture at Ohio State and also Bachelor of Arts at Capital, while our father was awarded the degree of Doctor of Divinity at Capital. For the rest of his life, Oscar enjoyed bragging about this. "The Lenskis got four degrees in one day, and me . . ." pointing to himself, "I got *two* of them!"

My degree carried with it a certificate for teaching in the Ohio schools and my parents assumed I would apply for a school and settle down to teaching. Since I was interested in art, they thought I would make a good art teacher, but the path of my destiny lay in another direction. I came so close to teaching in 1915 and several times later when good offers were made to me, it is remarkable that each time I evaded it and chose another path. Teaching would have brought me the contacts with children which I instinctively wanted and was looking for, but always another star loomed over the horizon, beckoning me on. I did not know what this star was or where it led, but I followed it blindly and with a sure faith.

In my art classes at Ohio State, one of my instructors, Louise Shepherd, began talking to me about going to New York to study art, as she herself had done. She knew of a good art school and of a branch of the Y.W.C.A. where students of the arts could live. I listened. Her encouragement was the first step in finding my chosen work.

I began to make my plans, but my father did not like the idea and opposed it vigorously. He said he could not help me financially, and if I went I would have to be entirely on my own. I was entering a field totally unknown to him, and he had heard stories of the dangers of living in the city, especially for a young woman. His whole desire was to protect me and he wanted me to choose something safe. Also he felt that I needed no more training, I had had enough and it was time for me to become self-supporting. Not until after Professor Charles Fabens Kelley, head of the Art Department at Ohio State, came to our home to talk matters over, did his attitude change and he gave his reluctant consent.

How I ever summoned up enough courage to make the break from home in the face of his disapproval, and embark into this adventure into the unknown, I do not know. I was sober-minded, timid, inexperienced, and had practically never traveled at all. But something inside was urging me on and I had to listen to it.

ART STUDENT IN NEW YORK 1915–1920

In October, 1915, I went to New York by train, having my first experience sleeping in a lower berth, arriving in the pouring rain. I was to stay at the Studio Club, a branch of the Y.W.C.A. for women students of art, music, and drama. Miss Evelyn Newman was director at this time.

Because of my limited funds, I was given a room in a "neighborhood house" on a side street. I well remember my first night in the big city and my futile attempt to get a little sleep through the raucous cacaphony of street and traffic noises that I was unaccustomed to and unprepared for. The Studio Club proved a wonderful anchorage during my student days in New York and I always enjoyed the associations made there and the opportunity to get needed help and advice.

Professor Kelley had advised me to study at the Art Students League and picked out my instructor there—Frank Vincent DuMond. As soon as I was settled into my room, I paid my first visit to the League. On the front doorstep in a crowd of newly-arrived students, all waiting to register, the first person I met was Mabel Pugh of Morrisville, North Carolina, who had also come to New York to study art. Agnes Lehman from Buffalo was another new League student, and she and Mabel became lifelong friends. We three had converged upon New York on the very same day.

DuMond was an inspiring teacher, but a very harsh one. I suppose I felt his criticisms so keenly because I had started so far back and had so far to go. Trying to learn to draw under his tutelage was a hard struggle. Later I studied with F. Luis Mora and Kenneth Hayes Miller.

I lived first in a "hall bedroom" on the fifth floor of a brownstone front on East 57th Street, one of the Studio Club's "neighborhood houses." My room measured 7 x 11 feet, and my furniture consisted of one narrow cot and one straight-backed chair. My trunk had to be unpacked on the second floor, and the contents carried piece-meal up the rest of the way. After a few weeks, Mabel Pugh and I decided to room together. We took a double room on the third floor of a house on a nearby street, renting from a baroness, who was a voice teacher.

Diary 1915

"The Baroness is enormously fat and very peculiar. She has been an invalid for six years and must have quiet, so that accounts for the fact that she can stand only two meek little artists like Mabel and me on the top floor. The room is a dollar and a half cheaper, so I can save by living here."

Mabel and I loved New York and were very happy there. We were fearless and went everywhere, exploring and sketching in our free time, spending many hours on Orchard Street on the lower East Side, in what was called the "pushcart section," with teeming humanity overflowing streets and sidewalks. Later I made oil paintings from some of my sketches. Besides making graphic records, I was also writing down my impressions of everything about me in my diary. I described scenes at the League, on the streets, in Central Park, even noting the styles and fashions of adults and children. That October the girls at the Studio Club were asked to march in the Suffragette Parade:

Diary Oct. 22, 1915

"I just got back from viewing an hour and a half's worth of the Suffragette Parade. The New York women surely deserve the vote, merely for having braved the arctic weather which has descended upon us. Everyone's nose was red and you could see how stiff their fingers were, except those who had their hands in their pockets. The whole city must be peppered with yellow balloons and pennants. The parade started with miles and miles of school teachers of every description, then all kinds of other females. I stood for an hour and a half, then gave up and came back, as I could not endure the cold even for the good of the cause. I am thankful that I did not march, as I doubt if the marchers are done yet."

Economizing was nothing new to me, for I had never had a chance to be extravagant. Other girls besides myself at the Studio Club and the League were living on a shoestring. Once when I was stranded in lower New York with an empty purse, I had to ask a policeman for a nickel for streetcar fare. None of the girls had any money, and we all had to think up tricks to save our precious cash. A single room could be rented for $3.50 a week, a double for five or six dollars. We took dinners only at the Club, paying $3.50 weekly. We ate breakfast in our room, cornflakes and buns, at one dollar a week. My letters of this period speak of "breakfast of cold cereal and fruit," "dining on fruit salad," and "bananas to fill up on." Once I wrote: "To avoid housekeeping, we are living on shredded wheat and fruit salad."

For four years my biggest problem was making ends meet. My bank account began to dwindle fast, with nothing coming in and everything going out. So instead of taking two classes a day, I enrolled in only one. For the other half-day, I felt I had to work. At the League there was always a bulletin board where want-ads were tacked up. Other girls as hard-up as myself watched these advertisements like hawks. Through them, we got jobs to help supplement our slender savings. For the four years that I studied in New York, half of my time was spent in earning money. So actually I had the equivalent of only two years of full-time study.

I worked for Gorhams, painting watercolors on minute engravings on their Christmas cards. I started at thirty-five cents an hour and was afterwards advanced to fifty cents. I never painted lamp-shades, the lowest form of art, the work that paid the least. For a long time I worked at the Norcross Company, then starting out in the greeting-card business. My coworkers were Helen Sewall and Grace Paull, both of whom became well-known book illustrators later. *They* were designing the cards, mostly old-fashioned Christmas scenes, with stagecoaches and carol singers, but I was not allowed to do that. I could not draw well enough, my boss told me. I did the hand-lettering of the message.

For another greeting-card company, I composed verses, for which I was paid one dollar each. I considered this easy money, for I wrote the verses easily. I could jot down ten verses overnight, take them in, and come home with a check for ten dollars! For a time, I actually made fashion drawings for an Ad-Cut Service. I had to draw a woman's figure in a certain suit or coat. I was supposed to go and look at models in shop windows and copy them, but I usually made them up. It was good practice in getting figures into lifelike positions. I tried to make them doing something instead of just standing and staring.

Many years later, in 1926, I wrote in a letter:

> "I came to New York in 1915 with only $300 in the bank and no one backing me at all, when I could not draw or paint either one. But I was determined to earn the money to study with and to keep on staying in New York. That first year I earned $500 and each year after that as much or more, studying half-days at the League all through it."

There was no choice. Had I not been able to earn and supplement my funds, I would have had to return home—to stay, and to take up teaching. But if my first year in New York taught me anything, it made me realize how much creative work meant to me and how important it was to get more training. It was the beginning of a creative urge that was never to let me go.

Flower Girl   That first summer, 1916, I did return home and was plunged deep into the flower business. At this time, my father's latest hobby was horticulture. He and several other professors at Capital were growing flowers. There was keen competition among them in the growing of giant gladioli and dinner-plate-size dahlias. They began selling cut flowers to the florists up on High Street, and my father followed suit. So I had a big job cut out for me. Besides becoming his main helper in the garden, the actual selling devolved upon me. I had to telephone the florists, tell them what flowers we had available on that particular day, take the order and then deliver the flowers. If one florist did not want or could not use them, I had to keep on telephoning to find those who did.

We had no car at this time and the only way to get to High

Street was by streetcar. The florists provided the empty boxes, and I had to carry them—those for gladioli were six feet long!—under my arms and protect them from other passengers in the long slow rides uptown.

My letters tell the story:

July 23, 1916

"I do not have time to get lonesome. I have to tend to selling the flowers every day, which generally means a trip uptown. Then there is a lot of work keeping the garden in order, hoeing weeds, sprinkling and watering—it is very dry here now—and cutting flowers. The sale is just starting now for asters and gladioli, which will be our biggest crop."

August 18, 1916

"The flowers have been very successful. The dry weather held them back, but for the same reason the demand was great and prices extra good, some twice as high as in other years. The gladioli are nearly done and the late asters are starting. I have taken in about $150 clear already, and the amount is increasing from $3 to $5 a day. There will be some asters and dahlias after I leave, but I think I can persuade the folks to send me the cash, as I shall need it."

That August I also wrote:

"That waist I had on in the picture is an old cast-off of Miriam's. I have acquired several such. She is shocked at me, thinks it's awful to go to New York and then come home and dress as I do, when sensible people go to New York just to get the styles! Well, I should worry! I intend to buy a new corset and make over that pongee dress and that's all. Oh yes, I made me a smock for painting. It's a beauty and I'm going to make another if I have the time. Papa paid for it—Hooray!"

The summer was not all work, however. With the two Stellhorn girls, Alma and Martha, Miriam and I played tennis with several Cap students every evening on the campus courts just across the street from our house.

"I never had more fun in my life. After the games we go over to the drugstore, where the boys come in handy with their change. Then we adjourn either to our house or to Stellhorns for an evening on the porch, A—— entertaining us with his mandolin or delighting us by breaking forth in song! I don't know when I've enjoyed myself so much or found such a congenial crowd. It's an atmosphere of real friendship, a thing I didn't even catch a glimpse of in New York. For this reason, I shall hate to leave here in the fall.

"I haven't had a chance to do any art work at all. I am excusing myself that it is too hot. I certainly wish that my old ambition would return, or something to make me get a move on. All my resolutions about 'doing things this summer' have vanished in hot air. I can't understand how I was ever so ambitious as to resolve them. Don't mention 'art history' to me—it makes my head ache."

A letter written in September, 1916, tells of a great temptation that came to me:

"I have been offered a position to teach in the Lutheran Academy out in Hebron, Nebraska, salary $90.00 a month and room free; also traveling expenses paid. I would have had my choice of subjects (no Art) and have charge of the girls' dormitory (15 girls). It almost turned my hair gray to decide, it was such a temptation, as I could have saved $500 or $600 easily. And it did take some grit to give up the chance of that much money. I talked to Miss Louise Shepherd (former Art instructor at Ohio State) for advice, and then gave it up. But I am not sorry for the way I decided.

"I talked to Prof. Kelley (head of Art Dept. at State) before I left and showed him my work. He told me all kinds of nice things, among them that after this next year in New York, I can come back to Columbus any time and take a position teaching at State! He also gave me some valuable advice as to what to do this year. So I feel fine, all ready to do big things!"

Back in New York I returned to New York that fall, enthusiastic and happy. My refusal of the teaching offer had made it plain that I *had* to go on with my art training. I knew well my own deficiencies and was determined to remedy them if I could. But most of all, I knew I could only be happy when doing creative work. My star was in the sky and I wanted more than ever to reach for it.

Mabel Pugh, my 1915–1916 roommate and companion, left New York and went to Philadelphia to attend the Pennsylvania Academy of Art, and did not return to the League. Most of the letter quotations that follow are from letters written to her over the ensuing years. In my second year I roomed with my cousin, Clara Lenski, who had come to New York to study violin.

Those first two winters, in addition to my half-days at the League, I also worked at a free night art class, held in a public school on East 42nd Street, called the School of Industrial Art. Several girls from the Studio Club were attending and asked me to go along. We worked in an Illustration Class taught by Arthur Covey. Here we were allowed freedom of choice as to subject matter and medium. There were no models. We were supposed to get ideas of our own, stories or poems to illustrate, and to make our own compositions. I worked on a set of nursery rhyme designs. Agnes Lehman and Mabel Pugh were in this class the first year and we got to know and like Mr. Covey.

That second winter, besides studying conversational French with a French woman at the Club, and swimming at the Y.W.C.A. twice a week, we girls had a good dose of culture. We went to hear all the famous New York preachers, and were given tickets to many theater performances. We saw Maude Adams, Laurette Taylor, William Faversham, and many others, never missing an opportunity. We spent many Sunday

97

afternoons at the Metropolitan Museum, studying the Old Masters as well as more modern schools of painting. How we reveled in it all!

In my spare time I worked on ideas of my own. Invariably they turned out to be pictures of children. I made up a portfolio of samples and started visiting publishers. Showing my Mother Goose figures resulted in my very first illustration work. Mr. Platt of Platt and Munk liked my drawings and gave me encouragement. He predicted that some day I would be well known, and was pleased to start me off. I received one hundred dollars for the *Children's Frieze Book,* a paper-covered coloring book of nursery rhyme figures, with a continuous landscape background. The child was supposed to cut the pages out and mount them on the wall in a continuous frieze.

There was always that bugaboo to face, the fear that I might run out of money and have to go home. But always something happened just in time. Mr. Platt continued to give me work. Other paper-covered picture books that I did for him before 1920 were: *Dolls from Fairy Land, Dolls from the Land of Mother Goose,* and *Mother Goose Cut-Outs.*

The impact of culture continued in 1917:

> "Have been visiting all sorts of churches and hearing various new ideas—Unitarianism, Ethical Culturism and even anarchism—I actually heard Emma Goldman! Heard Billy Sunday twice, but did hit the sawdust trail."

> "Sat beside John D. Rockefeller in church today. He looks just like his pictures, though not so feeble! Watched to see if he would put a dime in the collection plate. It was a bill, but I couldn't see how much."

I was still working in the Covey Illustration Class.

March 12, 1917

> "Mr. Covey is as stuttery as ever. He has been pricking up his ears and taking a little notice of me lately, to *his* surprise.

Lovrein Price, Sybil Emerson, Hugh Spencer, and Agnes are all in the class now."

". . . at night school last night, Mr. Covey was not there. We all heard of the death of his wife after the birth of a son. What will he do with those two youngsters—big, awkward, helpless man that he is!"

I had an offer to teach crafts at a girls' camp in New Hampshire for the summer of 1917. So I wrote:

"I am planning not to go home this summer. I can't bear to go back to flower-peddling and give up all art work for housework as I did last summer. As for the money, I feel the family thought I didn't deserve it, as they had to do the hardest part of the work before I got home. Then, too, Miriam needs some compensation for having to stay at home and manage things all winter long."

At Camp Tahoma, Pike, New Hampshire, I taught basketry, woodblock printing, and embroidery. I was supposed to include pottery, but could not as I knew nothing about it. My teaching took two hours a day. There were forty girls, three sharing my tent with me. We went on hikes and canoeing trips, played tennis, and Professor Luehring of Princeton University, swimming counselor, taught me to swim the first week. I was promised time for outdoor sketching, but did not do much. I helped the girls put on charades and all kinds of skits for entertainments in the evening. This was a lot of fun. I found the summer very healthful and refreshing—and had fifty dollars in my pocket to take back to town with me.

Mural Assistant   In November, 1917, I moved to Brooklyn, on the advice of a former Studio Club friend. Some rooms were for rent in a house next door to a private school, retained as a home for some of their teachers. I had a large, double second-story room with windows on three sides, overlooking a backyard with grass and trees. I was allowed cooking and laundry privileges and could keep the same room over the summer, returning to it in the fall. The rent was lower, too—always I had to think of cutting corners and saving pennies. It was fortunate that I had free tuition at the League, a secret scholarship used for needy, deserving students.

Work continued to come in. Mr. Platt continued to like my work and once told me he thought I "would go far." I did a series of ten color plates for *Grimms' Fairy Tales* and another ten for Andersen's. I saw the proofs of my Nursery Rhyme coloring book, and decided "it's not half bad."

November 1917

"Yes, I'm back with Mr. Covey in night class and he has been kind enough to give me the chance of being his assistant . . ."

Mr. Covey was working on murals for Lord and Taylor's Christmas toy shop. The subjects were nursery rhymes, "The Old Woman in the Shoe," and many others, dolls, toys and games, Eugene Field poems, and fairy-tale characters. Also to be done were some romantic landscapes with castles and moats, backgrounds for fairy-tale characters and episodes from Gulliver's Visit to Lilliput.

"Not being able to do children, and it being a rush order, Mr. Covey got me to help and used my designs almost entirely. I did all the drawing while he followed up with the big flat washes, then we both refined. It was lots of fun, but very hard physical labor, from crawling up step-ladders to sitting on the floor and jumping up and running back to see the effect."

At this time my brother Gerhard was a Chaplain in the Navy and often made stopovers in New York. In March, 1918, he was stationed at Brooklyn Navy Yard, awaiting sailing orders between his many trips across the ocean to France on troopships. He was very handsome in his spotless white uniform and gold braid. All the girls at the Studio Club envied me my good-looking escort, not realizing he was my brother. He and I often went to concerts and the opera together. One high spot was hearing Caruso in *Samson and Delilah*. Knowing that I was living on a shoestring, Gerhard often slipped a ten- or twenty-dollar bill in my purse, for which I was most grateful.

These were happy days with Gerhard. We established a lasting friendship and respect for each other, based on mutual literary and artistic interests.

Dark Days   1918 was my most difficult year.

In April, Mr. Covey left night school and started classes for men in camouflage in New Jersey. That month I was offered a position at Brearley School, as assistant in the Art Department, four days a week from 8:30 to 1:00, with a large (to me) salary, large enough to allow me to have a studio very near the school.

(Letter)

April 14, 1918

"Brearley is a private school at 61st St. and Park Avenue, and is attended by Gould and Rockefeller youngsters. The offer sounded lovely and I nearly turned gray over-night trying to decide. However I turned it down—just like that! I refused it in spite of Mr. Covey's and everybody else's advice to take it by all means, But since I turned it down, I haven't had a single regret, so I think that's a good sign."

Had I been able to foresee the dark days that lay ahead of me, I might have made a different decision.

My stay in Brooklyn came to an abrupt end, due to a fire in my room, caused by my own carelessness. During a brief absence, I had left some clothes drying too near an open gas heater. The fire was not serious, was discovered and put out promptly and so was confined mostly to furnishings. Many of my books got their bindings singed to my great regret. When I came back from camp in New Hampshire that summer, the burned-out Brooklyn room was just as I had left it—impossible to live in. So once again I was out of a home. I soon reached my lowest point.

(Letter)

Nov. 30, 1918

"I packed up over-night and moved back to New York. At that time I had every confidence that things were coming my way, as I never hesitated in moving in with Miss A—— in her studio on 59th street and in expecting to return to it when she left the last of September.

"But before I had been there a week, I began to visit publishers and found to my utter dismay, that I would not be able to earn a single cent, because of restrictions caused by the war. So my prospective income vanished in smoke and I nearly vanished myself with the blow! I decided at once that a $40 a month studio was not for me, so I went on a search for something else. I walked the streets day after day and couldn't find a blessed thing. The Club was not able to help me, nor anyone else. I was nearly desperate, I thought seriously of going home —especially when Miss A—— moved all her things from the studio, including the bed which she had been letting me use. I had to beg and implore Mis F—— at the Club to take me in. I was there for two weeks, and during that time, happened upon Mr. Covey who came to my rescue with a nice job, and then through Miss A——, another fell into my lap, so things began to look a little more cheerful.

"Then I found an apartment which I was finally able to convince Clara that she must take with me, at 25 W. 16th St., at $75 per month—and no furniture. Which is where we have been living ever since.

"Mr. Covey wanted me for more work at Lord and Taylor's and wanted me to start in at once for all day. But this other job was afternoons only, so he was kind enough to let me substitute evenings for afternoons, so I could work at the gift shop job, at The Treasure Box in Greenwich Village."

The new apartment was very nice. Clara and I had separate rooms and cooked on an electric grill in the closet. But I had no idea how I could ever pay my share of the rent. Clara had a dependable secretarial job, with a regular pay envelope.

That fall I did not enroll at the League. Armistice Day came and Mr. Covey and I walked over into the cheering crowds on Fifth Avenue, celebrating the event. The war was ended, but publishing prospects were no better. I was fortunate to have the painting job with Mr. Covey. Again he was working on Lord and Taylor's toy shop Christmas display and needed my help. I worked with him mornings and evenings. From 12:30 to 6:00 P.M. I worked at The Treasure Box, clerking.

The work with Mr. Covey lasted for ten strenuous weeks:

"I painted fifty feet of the panorama all by myself! I worked right along with Mr. Covey through it all—planning original compositions, stretching those enormous canvases, drawing in with charcoal and then painting. It was certainly a valuable experience. Mr. Covey let me paint all the children! He has been awfully good to me and is now giving me as much credit for the finished product as he is keeping for himself. We have come to be very good friends. I can hardly imagine him as he used to be at night school."

All that fall, my day's program was a heavy one, from 8:00 A.M. to 10:00 P.M.—too heavy, for I soon paid the price. Both jobs ended suddenly and it was well they did. In December I came down with influenza. It was the time of the widespread influenza epidemic that took so many lives. I was taken to the New York Hospital, only a short distance from where I lived, where I occupied the last empty bed in a crowded ward, and was very ill. After I improved, I was taken to the home of the Rev. F. H. Meyer in Fordham, old and devoted Ohio friends, who cared for me like one of the family. Their home had been a second home to me, for Clara and I spent all our Sundays and holidays with them. Here I had a relapse, developed diphtheria, and was given antitoxin. I had a long slow recovery. This illness was the start of a lifelong battle for good health.

But several things happened to cheer me up. One of my oil paintings, "The Fire Escape," was accepted by the National Academy of Design and hung in their annual show. Gerhard, now stationed at Newport News, came to New York and saw my painting and liked it immensely. Of course, getting a picture hung in the Academy was the nth degree of achievement to all of us struggling art students. No wonder I was set up. Another thing that made me happy was seeing several of the paperback picture books I had done for Platt and Munk on sale at Brentano's. After leaving the Meyers . . .

> "I came back here to the apartment and for two weeks had to take things pretty easy, resting often, taking a tonic and doing no work. Since then I have gradually worked and gone about until now I am feeling just like new. I come and go like always without tiring more than usual, and have started back to work. I've just been doing my own things. I would like to be able to afford to do nothing else for the rest of the year, getting ready for what I hope will be a grand rush among the publishers next winter. But I can't think of that because of all my extra expenses this winter, the high rent, hospital, etc. So I've got to get some money somehow. I had hoped to be helping Mr. Covey again, but his project has been very much delayed for various reasons, and I am still waiting for word. And in the meantime I am canvassing the town for a job."

All I could get was a few temporary shifts with Mr. Covey on some fairy-tale panels, a few designs and some verses to be lettered for a greeting-card publisher. I was really hard up and scraping pennies now, but still I hung on.

That summer, 1919, Mr. Covey offered me work if I would come to Morristown, New York, for two months. He was to decorate the Infants' Wear department of Lord and Taylor, work he should have had last January. I went with him and we worked seven hours a day in the barn at Charles Chapman's ancestral homestead on the St. Lawrence River. A large painting of *The Pied Piper of Hamelin* was done in three parts. While working on the rat scene, I wrote, "I am feeling very ratty!" Also six smaller panels depicting details of a child's day—Getting-up Time, Meal Time, Play Time, Story Time, and Bed Time. I designed and executed them all. "Can you see me doing any loafing?" I was getting plenty of experience drawing and painting children.

Mr. Covey had his two children, Margaret, 10, and Laird, 2, with him there under the care of Emmy Rusack, another student of his. The menage was a strange one:

> "The place belongs to Mrs. Chapman, Sr., with whom Mr. Covey shares housekeeping expenses. I see practically nothing of the children as I am kept so busy. I get a swim and a row daily and that's my only diversion. Mrs. Chapman keeps open house, regular old-fashioned hospitality, and we sometimes have twelve or thirteen at table—all kinds of funny old ladies, and some not so old but even funnier. There's a young Irish cook, also with a child, red-haired, so it's a funny mixture. Most of the time Mr. Covey is the only man on the place . . . I sometimes get a banana-split over at the village, but aside from that, my life is very dull. I even see very little of this constantly changing household."

I had work off and on with Mr. Covey that fall and, after he acquired a new Ford, an opportunity to meet some of his artist friends, Charles Livingston Bull, J. Scott Williams and his wife Elsene Peck, who drew children, also Peter Newell, author of *The Hole Book.* They lived in New Jersey, where Mr. Covey's children were staying with a housekeeper.

Not until December was I able to enroll again at the League, this time taking Life under Boardman Robinson. In my spare time I worked on "ideas for books." I had only the vaguest idea of what a child's book should be, I was only feeling my way. I made a number of tentative dummies in 1919–1920—all very bad, most of which I burned up later. But I was continually drawing children and children's activities. Every picture I drew was of or for children, every verse (I did not attempt stories) was about and for children. Not that I had a definite idea of becoming a children's author —I did not aspire that high. I drew what I enjoyed drawing most, and unconsciously, without my realizing it, everything was leading me in one direction.

In the summer of 1920 I again assisted Mr. Covey, this time in Gloucester, Massachusetts, a place of which he was very fond, and where he had made special arrangements for the children. I had a busy time, combining assistance on his murals with dips in the ocean.

(Letter)

Gloucester, Mass.
August 14, 1920

"This is the most interesting town I've ever been in and presents a wealth of subjects for painting. All my spare time has been spent sketching in pencil and oils. I've done some landscape painting, my first real attempt, and the results have been better than I had hoped."

In June, 1919, Mabel Pugh was awarded a Cresson Scholarship at the Pennsylvania Academy, for a year of study and travel in Europe. Her actual departure was delayed because of war conditions, but we carried on a lengthy correspondence about it. I got the idea of going, too, so that we could travel together. Through the summer of 1920 I began to make active plans.

During my four student years in New York, my sister Esther and her husband were living in Perrysville, Pennsylvania, a suburb of Pittsburgh. Each time I returned to Columbus from New York by train, I made a stopover at Pittsburgh to visit them. Esther had three children, Gerald, Jean Lois, and Elizabeth Anne, of whom I was very fond. Often Esther would be ill and I had to take over, doing sewing, cooking, and housework, even canning. Hers was like a second home to me and the children afforded me constant delight. In February, 1919, Esther's fourth child, a boy, Jonathan, died at the age of four months. I made a hurried trip from New York to be with her, and was glad that I did, as none of the rest of the family could come, due to their concern over the condition of our little Grandma Young, who soon died after a long illness.

ART STUDENT IN LONDON 1920–1921

In October, 1920, I sailed to London on the *Finland* of the Holland-America line. I felt that a turning point had come in my life and I wanted a change. I chose London instead of Paris, the mecca of most art students, because I knew I would have to work to supplement my meager bank account of eight hundred dollars, and I did not want to face a language barrier. I had vague plans for staying a year or two abroad, if I could finance my stay.

Through a friend I heard of a furnished studio to rent, which I took immediately. While it was attractive and convenient, being located on Sloane Square, it was on the ground floor and had no central heating. I had to feed shillings into a metered gas stove, which barely took the chill off. The floors were stone cold and I developed chilblains which I had not had since I was a child. I was sure I had never been so cold in my life. In November came the horrible London fogs, which made it impossible to be out on the streets, and which even penetrated the room.

I enrolled at the Westminster School of Art and spent mornings there painting the figure under Walter Bayes, instructor. Most of the students were beginners. The war had kept people out of the art schools for four years, so there were no advanced students as I had hoped. I also visited publishers:

> "I am trying out the book field here . . . I went to a publisher the other day, and much to my surprise, was practically given a book to do before I'd been there ten minutes. It was John Lane, The Bodley Head. I was so astonished I could hardly believe it. You see, I've gotten so used to having New York publishers hum and haw around and never give you a chance . . ."

The book was *The Green-Faced Toad* by Vera B. Birch. I submitted sketches first then went ahead, using a line drawing technique in colored inks, which came out most attractively.

Although I had school work and a job to do, I was bitterly lonely. The English students were cold and let me severely alone. I found them unapproachable, with one or two exceptions. Mr. Covey had given me introductions to his late wife's relatives, whom I called upon and who were kind. But I had no real companionship, such as I had enjoyed from the beginning in New York. Then, too, I was unwell, suffering from a rundown condition, no energy and steady loss of weight. I went to a "panel doctor" and told him my symptoms. He said, "You are probably anemic," and gave me a bottle of "tonic" to take.

In midwinter, I gave up my handsome studio and moved to Bedford House, run by the Y.W.C.A., for two reasons—to save money and to find companionship. A room with meals cost me seven dollars a week, about half the cost of the studio, and I had no cooking to do, being introduced to a heavy vegetableless English diet. I longed for fresh fruits and salads, but never got them. My so-called "room" was a cubicle, with walls partway up to the ceiling. I could not see the girls in the other cubicles, but I could hear every word they said. It was not exactly my own idea of privacy, but there was no choice. Listening was a good experience in trying to understand the clipped English tongue and the English character. I was an unofficial and invisible observer, an ideal arrangement for a writer-to-be, who always had a notebook handy.

But I did not achieve the longed-for companionship.

I spent all my holidays and spare time at the art galleries and museums, studying Italian painters particularly, in preparation for Italy, where I very much wanted to go. I made a copy in oils of a painting called "Summer" by Puvis de Chavannes, whose work I greatly admired.

By February, I was illustrating my second book for John Lane, Kenneth Grahame's *The Golden Age*. *Dream Days* followed, but was not completed until after I had returned to the States. I made sketches for Thackeray's *The Rose and the Ring,* another publisher was interested, but nothing came of it. I remember how strange it seemed when I called upon an editor, to be offered a cup of tea before I opened my portfolio! I kept on working hard:

> "I want to do enough work here to have enough of a reputation when I return, so I won't have to begin at the beginning again with New York publishers. In other words, I hope the New York publishers will take me on without question."

In March I was invited by a middle-aged English woman to accompany her on a trip to Italy. I decided to go, as I was a bit fearful of traveling alone. This meant giving up Paris, which I had wanted badly to see, but it gave me three months in Italy and I loved it dearly. I roomed at Catholic convents in the towns where I stayed— —simple rooms with cold brick floors and no amenities. I took Berlitz lessons in Florence and picked up a few Italian phrases, so I could get around and make my wants known. I went by auto-bus to the hilltowns of Siena and Assisi, where I filled several sketchbooks. I loved the beautiful countryside, flowers and trees, the cities and villages so rich in art treasures.

In mid-May I sailed back to New York on the *S.S. Providence,* French Fabre line. I remember yet the wonderful taste of fresh grapefruit for breakfast, the first I had had since leaving the States. Mabel Pugh did not get to Europe until after my return, so we had our trips independently and never met there as we had hoped to do.

THE TWENTIES

PERSONAL 1921–1929

Marriage Two weeks after my return from Europe, I was married to Arthur Covey.

(Letter)

June 10, 1921

"I have been making up my mind for many months now, and at last have taken the fatal step . . . I just couldn't help it. I felt I wanted it more than anything else."

From Rome, on April 29, I had written to my sister, Esther:

"I hope to relieve him (Arthur Covey) of a multitude of details which have been keeping his mind off his own work. Do not think I intend giving up 'my career' as you call it. I intend to go on with my work much the same, but I hope to prove that a woman (or at least this one woman) can do two jobs at once!!! However, I may fail, I know that, and I am prepared for it, but I am willing to risk it. I know I am taking on the hardest job that any woman can possibly take on, but I believe all my sacrifices will have equal recompense.

"The last thing he wants is for me to give up my work and, of course, whether I have to give it up or not will depend entirely on him. But I have the greatest faith in him as well as the greatest love, so what else matters?

"I've come to believe that if there is some one who really cares, then nothing else matters—anything can happen; sorrow and trouble only deepen real love. But when you are alone and nobody cares—then everything matters and life is not worth living. I know more of that than you think, and that is why I cannot let love pass me by when it has actually come to me."

> Bearskin Neck
> Rockport, Mass.
> June 26, 1921

"I must admit my new title, Mrs. Covey, seems very queer. I feel very much as if I had lost my old identity somewhere and taken on a new one. I'm glad I have a sort of holiday summer up here in which to get used to it. Mr. Covey and I are alone, you know. The children are both on a summer's visit with relatives, Margaret with her great-aunt in Chicago and little Laird on a farm up on the St. Lawrence River. We felt that this was necessary in order to get things adjusted. The poor babes have been so tossed about from pillar to post that it is pitiful—and it will be difficult to pick up the few remnants of the old home and get things in decent shape for them before winter."

(Letter)

> August 28, 1921

"Life is serene in Rockport, only an occasional flourish when my husband brings in his morning sketch, or when the 99th of my 100 sketches turns out to be worse than usual. For the first time I am doing concentrated outdoor sketching. But I must confess the results are not what I might wish for. I seem to be in a muddled state of mind.

MARIETTA AND RICHARD LENSKI,
LOIS'S PARENTS, IN 1888,
THE YEAR OF THEIR MARRIAGE.

GRANDMA YOUNG, 1910.

R.C.H.L. PHOTOS

GROSSPAPA AND GROSSMAMA LENSKI, 1900.

LOIS, 1897.

LOIS, 1899.

R.C.H.L. PHOTOS

LOIS IN AN "ARTISTIC
POSE" WITH "FLOWING HAIR."

LOIS AND MAMA.

R.C.H.L. PHOTOS

PAPA WITH HIS CACTUS
COLLECTION.

ESTHER, LOIS, OSCAR,
AND GERHARD WITH
PAPA'S CACTUS
COLLECTION, SPRING-
FIELD, OHIO.
R.C.H.L. PHOTO

OSCAR, LOIS, AND
ESTHER LOOKING
THROUGH PAPA'S
BIRDCAGE.

"THE ANNA HOUSE,"
THE LUTHERAN PARSONAGE, ANNA, OHIO, 1905.
LEFT TO RIGHT: ESTHER, MAMA, MIRIAM,
OSCAR, LOIS, GERHARD, PAPA.

"THE GLORIOUS FOURTH," ANNA, OHIO, 1901.
LEFT TO RIGHT: MIRIAM, MAMA, LOIS,
OSCAR, MRS. NAGEL, GERHARD, WILL NAGEL.

R.C.H.L. PHOTOS

FAMILY PORTRAIT, ANNA, OHIO, 1907.
LEFT TO RIGHT: PAPA, GERHARD,
LOIS, MAMA, OSCAR, ESTHER, MIRIAM.

PAPA, LOIS, AND MAMA; TINTYPE
TAKEN AT SHELBY COUNTY FAIR, 1910.

LOIS AT HER HIGH SCHOOL
GRADUATION, SIDNEY, OHIO;
JUNE, 1911.

ARTHUR COVEY, 1919.

LOIS, 1919.

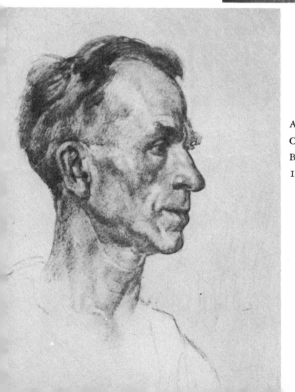

LOIS AND ARTHUR COVEY
ON DECK OF COTTAGE IN
ROCKPORT, MASS., IN 1921,
THE SUMMER THEY WERE
MARRIED.

ARTHUR COVEY;
CHARCOAL DRAWING
BY EUGENE SAVAGE,
1932.

971 SPLIT ROCK ROAD, PELHAM MANOR, N. Y.,
WHERE THE COVEYS LIVED FROM 1921 TO 1929.

LOIS WITH HER STEPCHILDREN,
MARGARET AND LAIRD COVEY.

LAIRD COVEY ON THE FAMOUS
"SPLIT ROCK," 1922.

GREENACRES, HARWINTON, CONN.,
HOME OF THE COVEYS FROM 1929 TO 1964.

A.S.C. PHOTO

LOIS AND SON, STEPHEN COVEY, 1930.

STEPHEN COVEY IN LOIS'S ROCK GARDEN AT GREENACRES.

STEPHEN, LOIS, AND ARTHUR COVEY, AND THEIR PET GOAT MISSY,
JUST AFTER LOIS'S RECEIPT OF NEWBERY MEDAL, 1946.

THIS BUILDING AT THE EDGE OF A HAYFIELD, GREENACRES,
WAS LOIS'S STUDIO FROM 1935 TO 1964.

CHILDREN'S PAINTINGS DECORATE
THE WALLS OF LOIS'S STUDIO.

"LO-LO" AND DAVID
CHISHOLM, THE REAL
DAVY OF THE DAVY
BOOKS, 1944.

LOIS AND ARTHUR COVEY, 1950.

LOIS,
THE AUTHOR.

A.S.C. PHOTO

LOIS,
THE ARTIST.

KEITH PHOTO

LOIS, THE GARDENER.

PEIRCE PHOTO

"Just now I am at home with my two kiddies, as Mr. Covey has gone to New York for several weeks in search of a home for us for the winter. He's having a very hopeless time of it, as New York and vicinity are so congested. We hope to be about an hour out of the city, by fast train connection, and to have a real house. That is *if* it can be found. We are both sick and tired of living in New York and refuse to try it again. Also it is absolutely necessary for the children to have a place to stretch their legs in."

The place he found was 971 Split Rock Road, Pelham Manor, N. Y., fifteen miles north of Times Square. It was the second fantastic house in which I was to make my home. It was a "gay nineties" house, with porches and turrets and a tower with a room in it; a winding stairway with three-sided balcony around the open stair well, over the banister of which I used to heave the heavy bags of laundry, letting them drop with loud thumps on the floor below, to the delight of little Laird. The house had circular sunrooms on two floors, and was three stories high in the rear, with the basement opening out on a lower ground level.

Had I been a writer of fantastic mystery tales, it would certainly have inspired me to scenes of crime or gory murder, as the house was a perfect setting for a thrilling who-done-it. Spooky plaster casts of weird-looking heads and abandoned dress-forms left in the attic by some previous occupant added to this impression.

While the house was a terrible white elephant, and difficult to care for, it had one advantage—plenty of space, and we soon spread ourselves all over it. The children had rooms of their own and a playroom, Mr. Covey used the downstairs sun parlor for his etching press, as an annex to the living-room studio; and I had an upstairs studio of my own, with a side alcove for a sewing room. The house had two old erratic hot-air furnaces, which consumed enormous quantities of coal and kept me running up and down the several flights of stairs to open and close drafts and dampers, and never succeeded in heating the rooms properly, but "the drafty old barn" as we called it served our purposes for eight long years.

Later, after he received an important mural commission, Mr. Covey was able to rent the separate studio building beside the empty stables in the back garden and transfer his work there, thus removing the smell of oil paint and turpentine from the house proper and giving us a more adequate living room.

Stepmother and Homemaker   I now had a new job, that of stepmother and homemaker.

Being a stepmother is never easy. If I had not known it before, the old fairy tales would have told me, for in them the stepmother is always wicked. Because the old tales are so unanimous in tone, it was evident to me that being a stepmother was a difficult, if not impossible job, in which most women failed. No story tells of a *good* stepmother, so the odds were against me from the start. This made it a challenge. I thought, what others cannot do, I will do.

All my life I had been surrounded by children. I was the fourth in a family of five. I had made playmates of neighbor children wherever I had lived. I always sought out children's companionship. So it seemed natural to me there should be children in my new home. The presence of the children was, indeed, one of its main attractions. Esther and my parents all had faith in me. They believed I would be a good mother.

I felt that the children's father had an impossible load and I wanted to help him all I could. I wanted to make a happy home for him, and give the children love and a kind of contentment they had never enjoyed. I was young and idealistic. In my relationship to the children, I sensed in a vague way that I would have to make up for the lack of a natural mother's instincts by cultivating a greater awareness of myself and them, in order to help them. And I had faith that it could be done. My biggest incentive, of course, was my desire to be worthy of my husband's love.

Margaret was twelve and Laird was four. I found them interesting, unpredictable, congenial, and companionable. I missed them when they were not there. I welcomed them when they returned. They both loved me from the start.

Not that there were no difficulties. I had been frankly warned by Mr. Covey's most recent housekeeper that they were "the worst children she had ever known." She told me how sorry she felt for me. She talked of their tantrums and continual disobedience, they always wanted their own way, they had never learned to do what they were told. But I paid little attention to these warnings. The children indulged in no tantrums and were not disobedient with me. I had confidence in my ability to get along with children, even difficult ones, and I felt I understood why these children had been difficult. My ideas of handling children were different from my husband's, for he belonged to an older generation, whose main weapons were pressure and force when they failed in persuasion. I could see plainly that his methods did not quiet the outburst but only increased rebellion and made the situation worse. It was years before he learned to trust me and stop interfering, and came to respect me for my stand.

Fortunately, I was well-trained from childhood in all the arts of homemaking—cooking, cleaning, sewing, and entertaining. In later years I often wished my mother had not done such a thorough job in training me. If I had not known how, I might not have had to do these things all my life. The actual management of our large house, the routine housekeeping, planning, ordering supplies, cooking, and cleaning was a big job. As early as 1922, only a year after my marriage, my diaries show that I was constantly tired and often ill, and photographs show me looking sad and worn.

Mr. Covey had a host of friends and loved to share his home with them. We were within easy and pleasant driving distance from New York, and other artist friends lived in nearby suburbs. So we were continually having company, not only for meals but also for overnight. Our house was a convenient halfway stopping place for friends in Connecticut on their way to or returning from the city. They often parked their children and their dogs with us, sometimes for indefinite periods. So a great deal of entertaining was necessary, and unless I had a maid, which happened only now and then, I was kept busy cooking meals for company.

I did a lot of foolish things, like putting in a garden to make more work. I knew how to sew, so I felt I had to make all the clothes for Margaret and Laird, as I had always done for myself. I also tried to teach Margaret sewing and cooking. Nothing was too much. I felt I could do everything, and the more I did, the more I was expected to do. I soon learned that it was all too much and that my physical strength was not equal to it. I had to resort to hired help. A succession of maids came from either New Rochelle or New York employment agencies, some for shorter, some for longer stays. One Danish woman, Helen Olsen, and her three-year-old son, Ole, lived with us for three years and became a part of the family. (Ole made wonderful drawings for me!) These periods of respite gave me a chance to recoup my physical resources and keep up at least a show of creative work. But the pressure of the household responsibilities remained heavy and took its toll.

I had continued the use of my maiden name for my creative work, for two reasons. First, because I had started with it before my marriage and did not like to make a change. It was hard enough to make one name for oneself, let alone two. Second, I did not want to be confused with other COVEY artists, both present and potential, since the children might also become artists. There had never been, to my knowledge, an artist in the Lenski family (nothing but preachers!) so I thought it was time to remedy that. I can never forget how our good friend, Fred Dana Marsh (father of Reginald Marsh, the painter) teased me about "leading a double life." When one of my housekeepers left us, Fred said, "I think it's a shame that when Mrs. Covey's cook leaves, Lois Lenski has to stop painting!"

When I was a young woman and an art student, in the years before 1920, there was considerable agitation and discussion about women's rights, and the whole question of career versus home. The question has never been settled, and is ever new with any woman who tries it. Let no one conclude that the combination of home and career is easy. Something has to give somewhere, as I quickly learned from experience. It may be true that a woman can have her cake and eat it, too, but she does not accomplish both without a struggle, and usually one side suffers if the other succeeds.

One day early in my marriage I complained to my husband that I had no time for my creative work, that the housework was absorbing me completely. To my surprise, he was completely unsympathetic. He replied: "Your job is the home and the children. They come first."

"But what about my work?"

"That's up to you," he said. "You'll have to find time for it."

I was overcome with surprise and anger, because he had always assured me I would not have to give up my work. My immediate reaction was rebellion. I said nothing, but I did plenty of thinking. To myself I said, "Very well, sir! I'll do it! I'll *make* time for my work! I'll keep it important!"

Actually, his remarks were good for me. They stiffened my backbone and made me determined to hold fast to my creative work. His words, in putting the responsibility up to me, in offering me no aid in my struggle, helped me to realize that I was truly possessed by this creative demon and *could* not and *would* not give it up.

I *made* time for my work. From that day on, I arranged the household schedule to allow me at least a few free hours each day, even if it meant doing housework in the evening after dinner, which my husband did not like at all. Fortunately, I had "a room of my own" to run away to. My studio on the second floor was my sanctuary. I would escape to its solitude, close and lock the door behind me, turning a deaf ear to doorbell, telephone, delivery man or outside interruption. Sometimes I escaped to exhaustion on the couch, but more often to my desk, where my beloved work awaited me. Here I entered a different world—a world of words and pictures of my own creation. Here I found solace for my spirit.

Things were easier if I had dependable help in the house, and I paid for such help out of my own meager earnings. I took advantage of such periods by "making hay while the sun shone"—making progress on whatever work was waiting to be done. But during the long periods of no help, I was submerged and often never got to my studio at all. It was always a battle to find time for my work, even after we moved to Connecticut. Maybe that is why it made me more determined than ever not to give it up.

I have often thought that I could not have lived through those first ten years of my marriage if I had not had a quiet spot to escape to, and the creative urge to bear me on, to bring me back to peace and tranquillity again, so great were the problems I had to face daily. I never, like many other artists, indulged in mood or temperament or sat around waiting for inspiration. My few hard-earned free hours were so appreciated, I could not bear to waste them. Every minute at my desk was precious. I learned to apply myself promptly to work in hand and to keep my work moving. My pleasure in it was the best incentive.

Those early years tested all my abilities as homemaker, artist, and human being. I was plunged at one jump into a sea of problems which only love, devotion, and determination helped me to meet, problems which most women do not face until after ten or more years of maturity which comes with marriage. I learned a lot in a hard school. But through it all, I had the joy and satisfaction of my creative work, which sustained and nourished me.

The Children Margaret Covey, or "Peter" as she had been called since babyhood, was a beautiful, intelligent, healthy, and talented girl. Twelve years old at the time I married her father, she always seemed more like a younger sister to me than a daughter. She was capable, independent, and self-reliant, and did not need me in the same way that her small brother, Laird, did. Then, too, she remembered her own mother vividly, and I respected this memory and encouraged it. I did not want her to feel that I was supplanting her own mother. She never called me "Mother" but "Lois." She benefited by the increased stability of the home after I came into it, although she did not realize it until much later. She had no influence on my work. (Later, she became a fine portrait painter.)

With Laird, however, it was different. He came to me at the age of four, when we were still at Rockport. His earliest memory of me is that I picked him up in my arms and carried him all over our cottage, upstairs and down, showing him his new home. During his four short years, he had been in the care of various housekeepers and had spent long periods in the home of Charles S. Chapman, artist, in Leonia, New Jersey. He had spent the previous summer on the farm of a friend of theirs, Caroline G. Craig, near Ogdensburg, New York.

Laird was very timid and full of fears at four. He was afraid of water. If I ran more than an inch of water in the bathtub, he screamed with terror. He was afraid of the new scooter we got for him. He would put one foot on it, but refuse to push with the other to make it go. He was afraid of the rope swing. When I set him on the swing seat, he would shriek at the top of his voice. Years later, he told me that goblin stories had been read to him every night at the farm, and had terrified him. Perhaps they were the seat of all his fears. It took many weeks of coaxing and patience to convince him that his fears were needless.

That first summer, Laird had only one accomplishment. He could sing a song that he had learned from Don Jones, the hired man at the farm. He sang it all the time until we got a little weary of hearing it:

> " 'Down by the old schoolhouse,
> Teacher stands by the door;
> Look in and see
> There's you and there's me—
> A couple of kids once more!' "

Laird was a little miser. He hoarded all sorts of treasures—every little stick, every little stone found on the beach or in the yard went into his pocket. His toy box soon filled up with sticks and stones, every one so precious it must never be thrown away.

Laird's bad reputation had preceded him. I not only heard vivid reports of his periodical tantrums, but I had witnessed several of them while he was in the sole care of his father. Somehow they did not worry me. From the moment he came into the house after I was there, all his tantrums ceased. He was always open to reason and suggestion, and I never, even in later years, had a discipline problem with him. In 1924, I wrote to a friend: "Laird is fine now, seven years old and the joy of my life!" He was indeed, a joy and a delight all through his growing years.

I never talked to him about his real mother, but his sister did. I did not want to confuse him with the idea of two mothers, at the age of four. What he needed to know was that having a mother meant being loved. I was intent on being a real mother to him. His father decided he should call me "Mother," because I was the only mother he had ever known.

Laird began to draw pictures when he was five. He made beautiful, sensitive, careful drawings of things that came within his experience. At Christmastime, he and I would play "Santa's helpers" and make Christmas gifts for the rest of the family. Laird made drawings which I put together into book form, one being a beautiful ABC book which he made for his father. Once he wanted to draw a cow, but could not remember what a cow looked like. So we took a long walk down our country road to look at one. Then he came back and drew it without hesitation. He could draw anything that he saw and knew. These early drawings of his aroused in me a keen interest in the creative work of all children.

When he was about eight, Laird announced that he was *not* going to be a mural painter like his daddy. No, sir! He was going to be like Uncle Charlie (Charles S. Chapman), sit out under a tree and paint landscapes. He didn't want to have to climb up and down ladders—that was hard work!

When he was in the third grade, he could not seem to master the multiplication table. The principal told me that if he did not learn it during the summer, he could not be promoted to the fourth grade. So I set about teaching him. I knew they used what was called "the product method"—as: $81 = 9 \times 9$. I taught him the multiplication table backwards and forwards and sideways all through that summer. He learned it, too. When I took him back to school in the fall, I went to the principal to report.

"If you didn't use the product method, all your time has been wasted!" she snapped.

Laird entered the fourth grade and had no trouble with arithmetic.

In 1924, I suffered the loss of my mother.

(Letter)

Pelham, April, 1924

"The month of April has been a very broken-up one for me and a very sad one. My mother died on Easter night. I was called home at the end of March and spent two weeks as night nurse. She was very low all the time, but rallied every few days. The doctor thought she might linger all summer, so Miriam came to take my place and I came home here to a rush of work—housecleaning, gardening, etc. I was here only a week when the news of the end came, and I had to make the second trip. You may remember that Mama had a stroke a year ago in March, and last spring I went out and helped to take care of her for six weeks. She has been a helpless invalid all winter. Of course, we could not wish that kind of life to be prolonged. But she was so young—only sixty. It is hard to understand why she should not have had ten or twenty more happy years."

Later

"I know so well what it is to give up one's mother and what an emptiness is left that can never be filled. But I also know the comfort that comes later, for my own mother seems closer to me now than ever, and I feel more vividly than ever the beauty and strength of our relationship. . . ."

PROFESSIONAL 1920–1930

Apprenticeship Professionally, the 1920's were a period of apprenticeship or preparation for my later work. In this decade I sketched incessantly, painted and exhibited water-colors, made linoleum- and wood-block prints, began illustrating for other authors, had my first one-man show of water-colors and oils, and had two books published. But all my efforts were learning efforts. I was still uncertain in which direction my work should go. Theoretically, I wanted and expected to be a painter, but practically, my experience led me into the book field.

I did not learn to draw at art school.

There were several reasons for this, one being that I did not spend enough time there. Even my half-days there were often interrupted for months at a time, when I had outside jobs to do. Another reason is that waiting until after college is late to begin. And, too, I had had few creative outlets in childhood.

After I left art school, I knew that I must learn to draw, and that I would have to learn without a teacher. So I began the sketchbook habit. I carried a sketchbook wherever I went. I took special sketching trips. I filled sketchbook after sketchbook with pencil drawings of people, landscapes, houses, barns, plant life—everything that came within my observation. This habit carried over into later years, after I began my Regional books. I filled sketchbooks as well as notebooks in every region I visited, so I obtained a visual as well as a verbal record of the area.

The sketchbook habit led to the notebook habit. I would observe not only the outward person, his action, his character, his expression, but I would also take the next step—I would notice what he said, remember his choice of words, his intonation, and most important, the emotion and motive behind his words. I first began to jot down his words in my sketchbook, then later carried a notebook for this purpose. My notebooks began to fill up along with my sketchbooks. This made for more character in my drawings, and after I began writing, helped me to put living people on the page in both illustrations and text.

This learning period, following after my student period, became an apprenticeship for all the work that followed. During these early years of marriage, I tried to reserve a portion of each year, a few weeks for a trip, perhaps, and to devote it to outdoor sketching, painting, and figure study, with the idea of becoming an artist, a painter.

I needed work on the human figure more than anything. Members of the Art Students League were invited to come to the League on Saturdays free of charge. Models were posing, many weekday students were absent, so the classes were small. This was a wonderful opportunity for me. I could go into any classroom and work where I liked. There was no instruction. I went and I drew. I drew both life and costume models, particularly the latter. I felt that clothes portrayed the character of the man, so I wanted to draw the man and this outward shell that protected him. I drew heads—I drew each model's head from many points of view, a dozen drawings, seeking, searching always for an understanding of basic form and character.

I made the long and tedious trip from Pelham Manor into New York regularly, Saturday after Saturday, for five years, from 1923 to 1928. My sketchbooks for these years show progressive improvement, looseness yet surety. I came to know and understand the human figure in a way that my previous art instruction had never taught me.

Equally valuable in this long learning-to-draw process was my constant outdoor sketching.

Before my marriage, in the summer of 1920 in Gloucester, Massachusetts, I had sketched and painted subjects that have always been my favorites—the town of little houses set on hills beside the sea, boats, shore-front buildings, piers and pilings, crowded beaches. But always—houses and people. In the spring of 1921, after my winter in London, I had spent three months in Florence and the little hill towns of Italy, sketching houses and people, houses of a different kind, with tile roofs on mountain sides. During the twenties, whenever I visited my sister Esther in Perrysville, I was entranced with this lovely city. A 1925 sketchbook shows beautiful drawings of Pittsburgh houses perched on its precipitous hillsides.

By 1926, I had acquired a sketching car, an Overland coupé, and had learned to drive. In half an hour, I could drive in the summer from our home in Pelham to Orchard Beach at City Island, where seething masses of humanity came out from the Bronx by subway to cool off, eat picnic lunches, and swim. Here I went whenever I could steal an hour or two, and here I found a real and never-ending panorama of human life to be studied. Many of these drawings were later made into wood-block prints and widely exhibited.

1926 was a busy year in this never-ending learning process. In April I went to North Carolina and in August to Provincetown, Massachusetts, an attractive town which had the same appeal as Rockport and Gloucester. There was the waterfront with docks, boats, and fish-houses, the town with little houses and church steeples, telephone poles, and streets with zigzag fences. There were crowded alleys with vistas to the waterfront, and patterns of houses, houses, houses. The sketches I made there were also used for linoleum-block prints, some for color wood blocks.

My trip to North Carolina was a real education for me. That spring, I was ill and worn with the strain of household cares and family. Mr. Covey had to be away on business, we made a plan for the children to stay with friends, and I was able to accept Mabel Pugh's invitation to come and stay for a month. She was then living at her old home in Morrisville. She wrote me that there was nothing to sketch there, so I need not bring my art materials. Did she expect me to sit around for a month doing nothing? I brought them, anyhow.

It was warm and pleasant in North Carolina, after the cold I had left behind. The very first day, from the front window of Mabel's studio over the local post office, where her sister Lessie was postmistress, I painted a watercolor of "Main Street"—a couple of country stores, a wagon and a car, a cow and a railroad crossing. (This was later reproduced on the catalog cover of my first one-man exhibition at the Weyhe Gallery in New York in 1927.) To Mabel's great astonishment, I found many things to sketch in her village, perhaps because I saw it with fresh eyes.

It was my first trip south and everything was new and different. I saw my first mule, my first gray-haired Negro, my first red clay soil. I heard for the first time a neighbor being called "Miss Lucy," and Mabel's sister was to everybody "Miss Lessie." I never dreamed then that I would one day be living in the south and know the thrill of being called "Miss Lois." I enjoyed hot biscuits and fried chicken for breakfast, drank raw milk from Lessie's cow, and gained ten badly needed pounds. On rainy days I sketched indoors. Here I found all the things I grew up with and loved to draw so much—oil lamps, footstools, ornate clocks, seashells, figurines on the mantelpiece, old-fashioned sofa, chenille table cover with tassels, iron cookstove and utensils, and geraniums in pots. (These sketches were later used in the making of illustrations for *Skipping Village*.)

Mabel and I took a sketching trip by bus. We went to Haw River, to Hillsboro and Greensboro and had many amusing sketching adventures. Once a fourteen-year-old girl came up to watch me draw, as I sat on my camp-stool beside the country road. I looked up at her and smiled.

"Out viewin' this evenin', ain't you?" she said, agreeably.

In the summer of 1927, Mabel and I took another sketching trip, this time to Chester County, Pennsylvania. Mr. Covey drove me in my little car through the New York and New

Jersey traffic to Byfield, where I met Mabel after he returned home by train. From there on, we explored on our own. We found a place to board and room in a small town, and traveled far and wide, painting barns, houses and fields, porches with house plants and rocking chairs and people in all kinds of activities. It was not always easy to explain to curious by-standers just what these two strange females were up to, but after a few words, they accepted us with amused tolerance. For the first time, they learned something about people called "artists."

Visiting Publishers I never had a literary agent, because I never thought of being a writer, and had no stories to sell. Even years later, after I was devoting most of my time to writing, I never had an agent, as I already had all my contacts directly with the editors.

I was an artist and wanted to sell my drawings. I had learned in art school that the way to get work was to peddle it—to visit the publishers not just once, but frequently, making the rounds from one editor's office to another as often as possible, sometimes seeing a special art editor or more often the children's book editor. Armed with a large portfolio of samples, you phoned for an appointment, unless you had already written for it in advance, and at the appointed hour, asked to be shown in. Because my portfolio showed mostly drawings of children, I tried to get book illustration to do.

A notebook kept at this time records my visits over a period of years and describes the receptions I received. I soon became accustomed to the usual alibis and vague promises: "Come back in a month," "Your work is very nice, but we have nothing along your line." "No new books are in progress right now." "Your work shows promise, but does not fit our needs." One male editor told me, "We have absolutely nothing on our fall list for children, I cannot look at your drawings because I have to catch a train." Another editor found my drawings "captivating" and asked me to leave my name and address. Another said, "I see you can do *any*thing. But we have nothing in hand right now."

As I look back now, I marvel at the editors' patience, when I think how often I visited them. I feel sure they were trying their best to fit me in. I enjoyed my visits with them, and while there was never a cup of tea and scones served as with the English publishers, we had enjoyable talks, some of which bore fruit long afterwards. A few were cordial in inviting me to return.

It was Helen Dean Fish of Stokes who said, "I like your drawings very much . . . but we have no manuscript to fit them." It was the same old story—my heart sank. Then she added, "Why don't you write a story of your own?"

A new door opened. It was a novel experience, after all the doors that had been closing in my face for so long. I did not know if I could write, but I wanted to try.

Illustrating for Other Authors   My persistence in visiting the editors brought results. Going the rounds year after year not only kept them remembering me, but kept me busy. I was soon offered various illustrating jobs.

I came into the children's book field at a good time. In 1920, after the First World War, publishing was just getting back on its feet again, and the publishing of children's books was starting in real earnest. At first there was only one children's book editor, May Massee; before long there were two more, Louise Seaman and Helen Dean Fish. By 1925, their numbers had increased and soon all the major publishers had special departments with special editors for their children's books. It was a good time for a beginner to start. I have been in the field right from the beginning. I came to know all the early editors because I illustrated books for most of them.

(Letter)

May 12, 1924
"I have been following up my book illustration work with New York publishers, for the first time seriously since I came

back from London (three years before). I found that the books which I did in London gave me an immediate introduction here . . . I am illustrating a book now for Macmillan, *The Peep Show Man* by Padraic Colum, and Stokes are considering one of my own with my own illustrations. (*Skipping Village.*)

October, 1925

"I worked from May to August on illustrations for *Chimney Corner Stories,* edited by Veronica Hutchinson, for Minton Balch. I feel it is a definite step in advance of anything I have done before. Also, I am hoping it may bring me more of the same kind."

In 1926, I illustrated *Chimney Corner Fairy Tales,* and in years to follow, others in this series.

In my student period and the early twenties, I was obsessed with the fascination of drawing medieval costume. I had long been in love with old English ballads, and in 1922 made a selection, with sketches, for a possible book, which was never published. In England, France, and Italy, in 1921 and 1923, I enjoyed the medieval tapestries, made a thorough study of them, then began drawing figures in medieval costumes, in various compositions, for my own enjoyment. In 1927, Dodd Mead published *A Book of Princess Stories* and in 1928, *A Book of Enchantment,* both compiled by Adams and Atchinson. In my illustrations for these books, my love of the medieval was given full sway.

Arthur Covey was a lover and collector of Persian prints, and we often visited the Anderson Gallery art auctions to make occasional purchases. This, together with visits to the Metropolitan Museum's Persian rooms, whetted my appetite for Persian design, which soon became another obsession. I had only one opportunity to express it, in my illustrations for *Rustam, Lion of Persia* by Alan Lake Chidsey, Minton Balch, 1930. I was somewhat astonished when reviews of the book mentioned the artist as being "an authority of Persian Art"!

My illustrating experiences were most enjoyable. Among the authors whose books I illustrated over a long period of years, besides those already mentioned, were: Caroline Emerson, Hugh Lofting, Cornelia Meigs, Phil Stong, Frances Rogers, Ethel Calvert Phillips, Dorothy Thompson, Lena Barksdale, May Lamberton Becker (*Golden Tales* series), Clara Ingram Judson, Mary Graham Bonner and Maud Hart Lovelace. Most of this work was done in the 1930's or later.

For Dodd Mead I designed many book jackets for adult novels, experiments in poster-type design. Some were frustrating, others a delight to do. I did not have to read the novel, was given only a brief synopsis, besides the title, and had to take off from there! Here, too, my knowledge of lettering came in handy.

In 1927, I enjoyed illustrating *Jack Horner's Pie,* a book of nursery rhymes which I selected and arranged. This was followed by *Alphabet People,* an ABC book with my verses, in 1928. Both were published by Harper's and designed by Arthur Rushmore.

I had some amusing experiences while illustrating for other authors.

Caroline Emerson wrote *Mr. Nip and Mr. Tuck,* published by Dutton in 1930. The editor arranged for the author and the illustrator to meet and get acquainted. Her book was a story of two imaginary animals, one of which had a spoon paw and a fork paw to mix salads. The other had a tail with a fishhook on the end for catching fish. I asked the author how she had visualized these animals. Were they large like elephants or bears? Or, were they tiny like mice? She had no idea. She did not know and she could not give me any suggestions. She had written the story without visualizing the characters. So actually, I had to *create* the animals in my drawings. It made me very happy when she was pleased with my illustrations.

I found that many authors are lacking in visual imagination. In certain manuscripts, I could find nothing to illustrate, I remember telling one of my editors that if nothing happens, if there is no drama in a chapter, then there is nothing to illustrate. An illustration must not be static, it must show action—something happening, not just people standing around talking. A story should be like a play, it should be drama, one exciting happening after another. This type of story is easy to illustrate and a delight to the illustrator.

In 1929, I had the amusing experience of illustrating a book before it was written. This was Hugh Lofting's *The Twilight of Magic*. His *Doctor Dolittle* books had been previously published by Stokes and were enjoying a wide popularity. These he had illustrated himself, but now he chose me to illustrate his new book. He came to visit me at my home in Pelham Manor, a dignified Englishman, and stayed for an hour, giving me a verbal synopsis of the first few chapters of the book. He described the characters and one incident. He talked freely as I took notes. He stressed the fact that the book was not to be humorous, but "a serious medieval story of two children who have rather mystical experiences." Mr. Lofting and I visited on our front porch, while my son, Stephen, then three months old, in his buggy nearby, cried intermittently.

In June we moved to Harwinton, Connecticut. Our new-old home was not yet ready for occupancy, so we boarded at a farmhouse in the village and I left the baby with a local woman as nurse, while I heaved furniture mornings, drew jacket, endpapers, and frontispiece afternoons on a borrowed card table. These drawings had to be ready for the publisher's salesmen to take out on their fall travels, so I had to make them before the book was written. It was scheduled to be published in August or September and the manuscript was to reach me any day. The author expected to finish it before he sailed to Europe in midsummer.

I waited. June passed and July passed. We got settled in our new home. In August I received word from the publisher that the author was sailing to Europe soon, the book was not written yet, but he would write it on the voyage and ship it back. The publisher would have it ten days after he landed.

My hopes rose. Ten days passed while the author was sailing to Europe, ten more days while the manuscript should be sailing back. Ten more days for good measure, but nothing happened.

In September, I visited my publisher, who said no word had come from the author. In November, a cablegram came from Czechoslovakia, ordering copies of the *Dolittle* books to be sent to a bookshop there. Winter and spring passed. My baby grew a full set of teeth and learned to walk. I heard nothing from publisher or author. June came again with roses and sunshine. I began to wonder if the book would ever be published.

Suddenly a long expensive night letter arrived unexpectedly by Western Union from California, signed by a secretary, asking me if I was the artist whom the author chose to do the illustrating, what drawings I had already made, and whether I intended to continue the work and whether I was at the same address. My affirmative reply brought no response. Again dead silence. Weeks passed, then the publisher sent word that the author was ill in Idaho. I forgot about the project and devoted the summer to gardening.

In July, 1930, another telegram came, this time from Arizona, saying the manuscript would be sent in ten days. *Are you ready?* Like the call of the Angel Gabriel on the last day, *Are you ready?* My answer, "Yes, I'm ready," seemed to produce a ripple. In two weeks an important document arrived by registered mail. I heaved a sigh of relief. At last . . . at last . . . but I spoke too soon. Upon examination, the type-written manuscript proved to be an exact copy of the first three chapters of the book, which the author had rehearsed verbally to me on that by now historic afternoon, our first interview.

The remainder of the story came to me a chapter at a time, from here, there, and everywhere, at intervals of about ten days through the rest of the summer. There was a long gap before the final chapter—did the author not know how to end the story? As each installment came, I placed it unread in a large envelope with the preceding ones. I did not read the manuscript until it was complete. This was necessary in order to get a unified idea of the story as a whole, and to choose the relative importance of various incidents therein and their relation to the whole.

I then made the drawings and the book was published late in the fall of 1930.

Skipping Village—A Beginning In 1921, Mr. Dominick of Stokes, on his annual book hunt in London, had found a book called *The Green-Faced Toad.* No one could tell him much about the illustrator, but he bought an edition for the American market largely on account of the illustrations. Not until he returned to America did he learn that the artist was neither Russian nor English, but a native of Ohio. All the people at Stokes were surprised when this illustrator walked into their office one day, unannounced! This was probably in 1922.

Because I had done some illustrating in London may have been one reason why Miss Fish paid particular attention to me. In 1924, I made a tentative dummy which I called *A Child's Town.* It was composed of verses and there were four full-page illustrations. They were pictures of people in 1900-costumes like those of my childhood. Miss Fish liked the drawings. But, horrors! One look at the dummy was enough! It would not do at all! It was written in VERSE! Rhyming had always been easy for me, so my thought was, why not give children some poetry along with my drawings? Oh, no! It would not do at all. Poetry did not sell. Stokes could not consider publishing a book of poetry, amateur poetry at that. Then she said, "Write a story about your childhood—in prose."

I went into action at once. I worked hard to turn my verses into prose, elaborating the ideas with remembered incidents of the various escapades of the Lenski family, and to make a story out of it. The prose version, when I brought it in, must have been a crude affair. Miss Fish pointed out many faults and gave me concrete suggestions, showing great patience, but asking for considerable revising. Still I did not get *too* discouraged, although I seem to have worked over it for two years before it was acceptable. I was loath to give up my verses, so I sneaked a few of them in, between the chapters.

(Letter)

Feb. 28, 1926

"My big news is that I am now an AUTHOR! I have just signed a contract with Stokes to publish a book which I have written called *A Child's Town.* It will not be out until next January and I will have until November to make the drawings. Stokes have made me promise to let them publish 'my second volume.' So I may have to be a writer in spite of myself!"

Galley proofs were read in October that year and the illustrations delivered by November. Blue cloth was chosen for the cover, the title was changed, and the book was published in late spring, 1927. It was *Skipping Village,* my first book. Although I was an author, I did not take it very seriously. I was still determined to be a painter.

I had to keep my promise to Stokes. The 'second volume,' *A Little Girl of 1900,* written more easily and confidently, which also told of my childhood experiences, with also a few verses included, was published in 1928. I deeply regretted that my mother did not live to read my first book. I know how much it would have meant to her, so I dedicated it to her memory. My father took great pride in my first effort, but felt that I had not stuck close enough to facts. He advised me not to be afraid of reality and to speak the truth, avoiding too much fictionizing, but the impact of his advice was something I did not appreciate fully until much later. Fictionizing was and continued to be the accepted standard in writing for children. My father continued to encourage me in my writing. He forgot that he had ever objected to my going to New York to study, and in later years, even took credit for it.

He enjoyed each new book that I sent him and boasted of my achievement.

In spite of having a book published, I was still determined to be a painter, and a number of things happened to encourage me. Through the twenties, I was sending watercolors to exhibitions. As early as 1922:

> "I sold my largest water-color, 'The Golden Age,' at the Pennsylvania Water Color Show. I was never so astonished in my life. I did not think my water colors were good enough to exhibit even."

When I had five paintings accepted at the New York Water Color show, I wrote:

> "I'm beginning to think I'm a real water color artist and have been missing my calling heretofore."

After I sold two at the Chicago International, I began to be really puffed up! Two oils sent to the Independent Show in New York brought me invitations to exhibit at six other galleries, among them the Detroit Art Institute and the Whitney Studio Club of New York.

These successes were preliminaries to my two one-man shows—oils and watercolors at the Weyhe Gallery in 1927, and watercolors at Ferargils in 1932. John Erskine bought an oil, "The Sewing Circle," from the Weyhe show. Several were sold from the Ferargil show. I was quite elated.

Surely now I was on my way to being a painter!

From Artist to Author   The change from artist to author was a gradual one. I do not quite know how it happened, except that I woke up one morning and found myself an author! I had never aspired or planned to be one. I had always wanted to be a painter. What a wonderful metamorphosis it was! I now had two weapons to fight with, two outlets of expression instead of one. How wonderful that they both went hand-in-hand!

From 1927 on, after the publication of *Skipping Village,* there was a gradual weaning away from painting, even though I was still exhibiting and occasionally selling, and had had my two one-man shows. I still had plans for painting when I built my Connecticut studio in 1935. I arranged for a north skylight, in order to paint a series of portraits of my Connecticut neighbors—the actual people were already chosen—an exhibition of which had been promised me by a dealer in New York. A brave start was made on these paintings, but the series was never completed, for illness intervened and I was obliged to do sedentary work. Writing took the place of painting, although I still remained the artist, illustrating everything I wrote. Finally the AUTHOR won out and painting ceased.

Giving up painting was a real sacrifice. For a long time, I felt I would some day get back to it. But books filled all my time and I didn't. My husband began borrowing tubes of paint and brushes, saying, "You're not using them!" I kept my paint box for years, then when Stephen began to paint, he "borrowed" it, also canvases, stretchers, and whatever materials he needed. After all my supplies had vanished, I knew that I would not paint again.

In illustrating for other authors, so often I had found it hard to be sympathetic to a story written by another person. My own stories were congenial material to illustrate. In them, writing and drawing dovetailed ideally. I visualized my characters as I wrote about them, so that by the time the story was written, the pictures were already composed in my mind and I could draw them with little effort. I learned that my drawings could say things left out in the text, and that meant the text could be kept very simple. Text and illustrations supplemented each other and made a happy combination.

I began to take more and more pleasure in my writing. Books had always been an important part of my life. Suddenly the making of books became terribly important, more important than painting pictures. Books were living things, they went into the hands of children, and if they were worthwhile, they would be loved and enjoyed—and they could help shape lives. While I early gave up the idea of being a teacher, I have remained one at heart, and instead of reaching a small group in a classroom, the influence of a book upon many children has been unfathomable.

In the early days my ideas were few, hard to arrive at, unsure. Now they came on wings, they were legion—if only one had health and strength and wisdom enough to put them down on paper. Always through the ecstasy there ran a deep humility. This power is not of one's own making, how clearly we saw that. This creativity is a Higher Power working through us. That alone can account for its persistence, for the fact that it pursues us so relentlessly and will not let us go.

How often has this been proven true! A lame and halting idea suddenly takes on wings and soars of itself, with no conscious volition of the mind. How often a certain character in a story, whom we intended to keep unimportant, suddenly steps out and becomes the hero. How often a new and better solution of the plot comes of itself, or a story takes a new, unplanned-for turn. How often do entire scenes enact themselves more vividly and meaningfully than we had ever intended. And so the use of our gifts becomes not a selfish pleasure, but the holding of a sacred trust.

THE THIRTIES

PERSONAL 1929–1940

Stephen 1929 was a memorable year for the Arthur Covey family and not because of the collapse of the stock market. Our son, Stephen, was born in New Rochelle in February and we moved to Connecticut in June. All the time we lived in Pelham we had been hunting for "a farm in the country." Every pleasure drive was devoted to this purpose. At last we found one in Harwinton, Connecticut, a small village six miles from Torrington.

Stephen's arrival is best described in my letters:

Feb. 12, 1929

"My little son arrived last Friday morning, Feb. 8, nearly a month ahead of schedule. He is very tiny, weighs less than four pounds, but the doctor assures me he has made an excellent start and has already begun to gain . . ."

June 23, 1929

"Through all the turmoil of our packing and moving, Stephen was a perfect angel, slept most of the time and was so good, as if he knew he should be! He has been gaining ever since he came home from the hospital the last week of April. These two weeks up here in the country he has gained nearly a pound. He weighs 9½ now, which is BIG for him."

We had bought the 113-acre farm at Harwinton the previous August. We gave it the name Greenacres, because of its wide expanses of meadow. The actual moving was a tremendous ordeal, for which somehow I found the necessary strength. Baby and I stayed at a home in the village, during the settling in, and there I was able to get good meals and much needed rest.

Although we had looked forward so happily to our big move to the country, I must confess that I had a sinking feeling when I learned that there was no electricity or gas, and we would have to start with kerosene lamps and a wood-burning stove for cooking. It was like going back to the Dark Ages.

This was before the days of canned baby foods, and, in our neighborhood, of even pasteurized milk. Mixing formulas was easy enough, but pasteurizing milk that comes straight from the cows was another story. To keep the milk at the required temperature for the required length of time was impossible on a temperamental kerosene stove. When the temperature jumped up too high, there was nothing to do but send to the farmer for more milk and start all over again. Then, because baby was so tiny, the doctor insisted on middle-of-the-night feedings, which meant warming bottles by a glimmering smoking kerosene lamp. I averaged about four hours of sleep at night, with no chance of making it up in the daytime. There was also the daily diaper-washing without benefit of a washing machine, and other problems to meet. But somehow I managed and was amply rewarded by seeing my little son grow and develop like a husky weed. He caught up to his normal weight by his first birthday, and soon he was an active small boy running all over the place and furnishing all of us much joy and delight.

His life was so simple, it could all be told in a few pictures, so I soon became picture-book-minded. In 1932 I made *The Little Family* for him, dedicating it to "S. C. age 3." It was his favorite book for many years, as it was and still is for many thousands of children.

At about this time, his father was painting a large mural in his studio. The canvas was so large that it had to stand diagonally across the room. The subject was "George Washington Taking Command of the Army," and Washington sat astride a huge white horse, much larger than a real one. One day Stephen came into the room to look at the painting. He stepped back, hands on hips, and tilted his head, looking up.

"Well, well!" he said. "It's a w-orse!" (horse).

Stephen, of course, grew up in an artistic atmosphere, where he saw drawing and painting going on all around him, to which he paid little attention. Once when he was four or five, he came home from visiting his friend Lewis, who lived down the road. He came tearing into the house, bursting with excitement until he found me. Then he cried out: "Lewis's mother *can't draw!* Lewis's mother says she can't even draw a straight line!" He was very disillusioned. He saw his own mother making pictures every day and had assumed that all mothers did the same.

I used to do all I could to stimulate his imagination, but it was not easy. If I said, "The crocuses are up too early! Jack Frost will nip off their noses!" he would reply, "They haven't any noses." Or, I would say: "If you don't drink enough water, you'll dry up like a leaf, and go flying over the housetop in the wind!" and he would laugh at me. But of course he enjoyed it just the same. Sometimes after he had gone to sleep at night, I would take his clothes and mend a hole or sew a button on, then put them back in place. Next morning he would notice it and ask, "Who sewed this button on?" I replied, "Oh, the little fairies came in the night. They like to sew buttons on." Stephen looked me straight in the eye and said, "I don't believe it. Fairies are only in books." Was he lacking in imagination, I wondered? Not until he reached nine did he become interested in fairy tales, then, for a year or two, he read nothing else, but when this flurry was over, as promptly rejected them.

When he was four, he and the little boys he played with had only one game that they played with invention and imagination. They played "auto." No matter what they had, wagon, tricycle, or scooter, it was always an imaginary automobile, and they pumped up tires, poured water in the radiator and were continually getting stuck in the mud. All this to the shrill accompaniment of all the appropriate noises. They played this game with variations, day in and day out, never tiring of it. As I watched them, I realized it was a fundamental interest of small boys. And so I made *The Little Auto* (1934). Stephen loved every word and every picture.

The other Mr. Small books grew and developed with Stephen's enthusiastic help and under his supervision. For all my picture books he became my censor-critic-advisor-and-editor to make sure I got each book exactly right. He not only gave me ideas and inspiration, but audience-reaction as well. I learned that if I could satisfy him, other children would also be satisfied; that if he loved one of my books, other children would love it, too.

Through all the years of his growing up, we shared not only the making of books, but the reading of children's literature. We had a regular ritual—every night after the supper dishes were done, we sat on the couch to read, book after book, many of them over and over again. At first I read them aloud to him, then after he started to school and could read, he read aloud to me. Sometimes we took turns reading. The sharing of many books with a child is one of the great joys of motherhood.

New Home in the Country   We had bought our new home, for thirty-five years to be called *Greenacres,* in Harwinton, Connecticut, in August, 1928. The house was in a very dilapidated state, having stood empty for four or five years. The carpenters, "Big Charley" and his helper, had been working on it spasmodically all winter, putting in modern bathrooms and other improvements, with infrequent inspections by Mr. Covey on weekends. June came and it was not finished, but we moved in anyhow.

Laird, by this time twelve, was the first person to sleep in the unfinished house. He remembered for many years how spooky it was there alone and how much courage it took. Mr. Covey insisted that we must move in to get the carpenters out! But there was no kitchen stove, so he soon remedied that. He went to Torrington and bought a secondhand wood-burning range, an old model even at that date! I was horrified when I saw it, and was never able to properly cope with it. He had failed to ask me what kind of stove I wanted. I made some feeble protests, but the stove stayed, I regret to say, for over fifteen years, and I cooked many delicious meals on it.

In the summers, I canned vegetables and fruits on the crazy old stove, using the overflow from the farm and garden. Whatever we could not eat had to be canned for winter use. My husband believed in the old-fashioned ways—no fruit could be allowed to go to waste, so it went into cans. I have often said that if all the jars that I filled were standing in a row I am sure they would reach around the world. The big blueberry swamp down by the brook, one of the best in the neighborhood, yielded a huge crop every second year—forty or fifty quarts at least, and oh, how good the pies, hot from the oven on a cold winter day! Not to mention quarts and quarts of tomatoes, pears, and peaches, as well as jars and jars of jelly and jam. Much or most of my canning, over the years, was done in the evenings after dinner, when I could expect the whole family to help. I learned to save my strength by doing my creative work in the mornings, postponing housework till the latter part of the day.

Yes, the old stove stayed, and so did the old icebox brought up from Pelham. (I hardly need say that my husband was conservative in many of his ideas!) It was literally an "icebox," a big box with a lid on top, into which we heaved fifty-pound chunks of ice, after hauling them on the bumper of the car, dripping as we went, six miles from Torrington. The road from the corner was still an unimproved dirt road in 1929. Many a time our car had to be pulled out of a mud-hole by a neighbor's team of horses. Snowdrifts, too, were a wicked story.

Often, in the 1930's, the cutting of the hay crop on our forty acres of meadow land, demonstrated the whole history of agriculture. In one field a yoke of oxen, in another several teams of horses, and in a third a sparkling new tractor, as three farmer neighbors took off the crop. During those early winters, the farmer up the road had to come on horseback through the high drifts to deliver our milk. One winter, 1934, we lived, I don't know how, through several days and nights of forty-below temperatures. Drifts most winters were piled higher than the tops of cars in the plowed roadway. All the country children, even those as young as four, were proficient on skis and snowshoes. They *had* to be!

That first winter we were without electricity and pumped all our water by hand. Even after electricity came the next year, the power was unpredictable and liable to go off at the slightest sign of blizzard or ice storm, both of which occurred frequently, for the winters were rugged. We always kept a half dozen kerosene lamps filled and ready for use, besides a supply of candles. When the pump froze up, we had to boil water on the kitchen stove to prime it and get it going again, just as in my childhood in Ohio thirty years before. I remember one winter, much later, in 1943, when we were without lights and running water for two weeks over Christmas. Alan, Margaret's son, then age seven, was with us and spent many hours happily pumping the old iron cistern pump in the wood-shed for his amusement, keeping all the pails filled. My prediction about the Dark Ages really came true.

That first Christmas, 1929, I wrote a poem and used it on our Christmas card. The card itself was a block-print of our new-old house. I wrote the poem on one of those wakeful nights, after feeding the baby, when I could not get back to sleep. I always kept pad and pencil on my bedside table for just such emergencies. My mind always seemed to be more creative at a time when I should have been sleeping. I jotted down, by the dim light of a flickering kerosene lamp, one phrase after another. The poem is humorous, but it was created out of rugged experience. We never kept horses or cows, but did keep chickens for a few years, until I rebelled at wading through knee-high snowdrifts to carry them *boiling* water! After that, we bought eggs from the neighbors!

CHRISTMAS IN HARWINTON

"The horse broke loose and ran away,
The cow wouldn't give any milk today;
The sheep have wandered and gone astray—
    But it's CHRISTMAS in Harwinton.

Sawing's hard work in the old wood lot,
It takes so much wood to keep the stove hot;
The pump's as likely to freeze as not—
    But it's CHRISTMAS in Harwinton.

The wind blows down the chimney flue,
The snow drifts high—you must wade through;
So get out your arctics and eartabs too—
    It's CHRISTMAS in Harwinton!"*

And what a happy Christmas it was, too! That one and all the others that followed. Perhaps having to work for it the hard way made it all the more enjoyable. We were not conscious of difficulties, and did not feel that life was over-rugged or difficult. We loved the old home from the start. We loved making it livable and comfortable, bringing the warmth and enthusiasm of family life back under the old roof. We were the third family to live in it in those 140 years that it had stood there. We wanted to be worthy of the people who

* *The Life I Live: Collected Poems.* Henry Z. Walck Co., 1965.

had lived there when it was new. So, one by one, year by year, improvements were made and it became truly a home.

The Story of a House   Greenacres was the third remarkable house in which I had the good fortune to live—for thirty-five years.

On the exterior it was a plain, sedate, white New England mansion of the 1790–1800 period, without the usual green shutters. Inside it had three stairways, four fireplaces, paneled walls with secret cupboards and wide oak and pine floorboards. There was a hidey-hole around the chimney on the second floor, entered only through a secret panel in a closet. We hunted and hunted, but found no treasure—not a single penny. The house plan was identical with other houses in the neighborhood of the same period—a small entry hall with stairs inside the main front door, north and south parlors on the sides and kitchen with two small end-rooms behind. A huge stone chimney, fourteen feet square in the cellar, was the great buttress of the house and provided the fireplaces. The kitchen hearthstone was very large, three feet wide and nine feet long, held up by heavy beam braces in the cellar.

The fireplace wall of the north parlor was beautifully paneled, but covered with many coats of wallpaper, when we first came. I had the thrill of discovering the presence of the paneling underneath, and tearing off the wallpaper to expose it. The room above the north parlor was also beautifully paneled on its inside wall, its paper covering having been removed. The floor of wide pine boards showed signs of little wear and the room could only be entered from the front hallway. It had evidently been "the ballroom" used only for special occasions.

The house was originally built by the Jonathan Balch family, and had been called the Balch homestead. The Balches lived in it for successive generations for more than a hundred years. The last Balch to live there was Old Shelton Balch, who died around 1900. He was a bachelor and was said to have been something of an eccentric. He pulled teeth and repaired clocks, using as his workshop the two-story building at the end of the woodshed. Here he kept a collection of many clocks, all ticking and striking at intervals, and he pulled the neighbors' teeth as need arose. He left a fine example of his handiwork in a frieze of jigsawed animals on the flashing of the south gable of this building. That he had a unique imagination is evidenced by his choice of animals to depict—roosters, cows, elephants, and peacocks side by side; and a galloping pony with a man riding backwards on the horse's rump, shooting an arrow from a bow!

After Shelton Balch's death, the Drake chapter began. The Drakes were active farmers and had three sons growing up. They did active farming, planting trees in the orchards and corn in the fields. This was in horse-and-buggy days, in the early nineteen hundreds. They kept five horses and many vehicles—wagons, buggy, top carriage, buckboard, and a two-seated business wagon. The young men used the horses for racing, sparking, and driving to town to see their best girls. Once a tragedy took place, when one son, Morgan, lost his right hand and arm in a piece of farm machinery. There were two fires in the house during their occupancy. The parents died, the place was sold at auction and bought by one of the daughters. It stood empty for a number of years and the whole place fell into neglect. It was waiting for a new owner.

This is the house that became the home of the Arthur Covey family in 1929. Major repairs were necessary, new sills had to be put in, the cellar walls and floor cemented, the old siding removed so the walls could be insulated and then replaced. We always felt it was worth all the trouble we took to restore it to a semblance of its original beauty.

We loved it from the beginning. Stephen and Laird roamed over and loved every inch of pasture and woodland, built dams in the brook, tree-houses in the trees, outdoor sleeping huts and tents, helped spray and pick apples from the dozens of trees in the orchards and rode the tractors and hay-wagons of the farmers who took care of the fields for us. In later years, Laird's son, Paul Covey, did the same things and loved the old farm as much as they did.

The old house was the scene of many happy occasions, vacations with the older children home from school and college, and visits from artist friends and Covey relatives on weekends. The very first summer, when Stephen was a baby, we had a carload of visitors for every single weekend, until winter set in. It was as if Mr. Covey had written or telephoned to everyone he knew, saying in his hearty way, "Come one, come all!" and come they did! The summers were ideal, never too hot, no mosquitoes, sometimes rainy but more often perfect, with the children laughing and shouting, gardening and lawn-cutting going on, fruit and vegetables to plant, pick, and can—plus visitors galore.

In my rock garden in the old rocky barnyard, I grew many kinds of rare and unusual alpine plants. Gardening was a great joy to me, affording relaxation from tensions and a welcome change from housework and desk-work. Although later I had to neglect it because of illness and the lack of physical strength, it remained a place of great beauty, affording me ample recompense for all the care and love I had given it.

Shelton Balch's old clock shop, with the second floor removed except for a balcony, served as Arthur Covey's studio, and here he painted his major murals from 1929 on. It had a very high ceiling with a high skylight, so that even on the darkest winter days, it was a fine place for painting.

During the New England hurricane of 1938, Arthur Covey and his assistant were so absorbed in their work there, so shut off from the world, they never noticed that the wind was blowing harder than usual, was tearing down trees and bending others over to touch the ground. Mr. Covey completely forgot to drive down to the little one-room country school which Stephen, then age nine, was attending, to bring him home through the storm.

I was captive in *my* studio, watching the gale from my wide window, fully expecting the little building to be blown over any minute and go bouncing across the fields like a tumbleweed, with me inside! I tried repeatedly to open the door, but could not because of the strength of the wind. I would have had to crawl to the house on hands and knees. Not until late that afternoon, when the winds began to subside, was I able to get to the house, to find Stephen safely at home, to my great relief. A kind neighbor, transporting his own children, had brought him right to our house door. When it was all over, Mr. Covey asked, "Was it a hurricane?"

My Connecticut Studio On the top of a high hill, at the edge of one of our hayfields, there was a little unpainted wooden building. It stood under some tall pines, and there were maple and willow trees close by. In the hayfield grew white daisies, purple asters, and goldenrod. Up the tall stone chimney at the side of the building climbed a Virginia creeper, a mass of brilliant red every fall. This building became my studio.

Originally it had been called "the coffin shop." The Balches had always been the undertakers of the town and here they had made pine coffins. Other Harwinton homes had "shops"— small sixteen-by-twenty two-story buildings in their back yards, left over from the small industry period of the 1850's— "clock shops," "hat shops," "gun and harness shops," where these products were made.

I had the building enlarged in 1935, after my first serious illness, feeling the need of a retreat of my own, away from the house and household affairs, a place for creativity and peace. A fourteen-foot addition was put on, with a north skylight for painting. But I did little painting there. I had not the physical energy to stand to paint, or even to sit on a high stool. I had to have sedentary work, which I could do propped up to a desk with pillows at my back. And so my writing began.

It was a lovely place in summer.

The walk from the house led past my rock garden, the big

old elm, some white birches, and a raspberry patch to the little back porch of the studio, where I would stop for a moment to look off to the blue hills in the distance. "I will lift up mine eyes to the hills . . ."

Inside, brown linoleum covered the floor, and bookcases, filled with books, lined the walls. After a number of years, all available wall spaces were covered with children's paintings in brilliant poster colors, a never-ending source of beauty and inspiration. Under the great, wide, high north window, which threw a soft light across the room, there were two large desks. One, my father's old desk, on which he did all his writing during my childhood, had a large drawing board on it, which could be tilted up and down. On the corner of the desk stood a jam-pot full of pencils, pens, brushes, knife, and scissors, and on the desk in great disarray lay erasers, paperweights, paper clips, rubber bands, and other miscellany. The second desk, a kitchen table, stood at right angles to the first and had my typewriter on it, also a special box made by Stephen with shelves to hold several boxes of typing paper, and on top a row of dictionaries. The revolving office chair could easily be moved from one desk to the other. To the left, under the window shelf, were filing cabinets, where letters and book materials were filed, readily accessible.

A fireplace was behind me, in the old part of the building, leading up to the big stone chimney. Over it hung my one and only mural, a bird's-eye view of St. Valery-en-Caux, a fishing village on the English Channel, where in 1923, when Laird was six, we spent the summer. A balcony stretched across the west end, used for storage and shipping materials. Shelves and a counter below it housed books and supplies. Other cupboards held my collection of old dolls, toys, and books, which I began to collect after our move to the country. These things were often put on display when I had visitors—groups of children, or teachers and librarians.

My collecting began in a roundabout manner. In the country, during those first fourteen cruel winters, I felt isolated and completely cut off from the rest of the world. All our neighbors "holed up" like bears and hibernated, so there was no companionship. I had to go back and forth from house to studio, or out to the mailbox—my only contact with the outside world—on snowshoes, since Stephen fought a losing battle with the wind, in keeping paths open. Through the mail, by advertising and later by writing a small column of my own in the *New England Homestead,* a farm paper, I collected old folksongs, children's books, toys and games, and many other things pertaining to childhood of the past. On our drives through New England in the summers, we made frequent stops at antique shops, so collecting became a side interest, and gradually stimulated my interest in writing historical books.

The studio fireplace did not give adequate heat for winter, so I installed an old six-sided wood laundry stove, which also was inadequate, even when converted to oil. The arched ceiling was high, and although the building was well insulated, it was hard to heat. Finally I achieved a hot-air furnace in the small basement, which did the job. The nineteen thirties were busy years. They saw the creation of most of my historical books, the creation of Mr. Small and the start of the Mr. Small series, and continued illustrating for other authors.

So from the little studio at the edge of the hayfield, at a time when I felt cut off from the world, a steady stream of books began to flow out to children all over the country, which later was to reach children all over the world. Although the years were lonely ones, as I worked alone, having no contacts at all with other writers, yet I was reaching my hand out and touching the lives of hundreds of thousands of children. For twenty-eight years, from 1936 to 1964, my studio was the headquarters for all my creative work.

PROFESSIONAL

Historical Books 1936–1944 After my first two books, which were stories of my childhood, Stokes expected me to continue. So, in the early thirties, since I had not yet developed any particular goal or ideal for my writing, I had first to feel my way by doing the usual thing—a group of imaginative stories for pure amusement. These were *Spinach Boy, Arabella and Her Aunts, Grandmother Tippytoe, Surprise for Mother, Two Brothers and Their Animal Friends,* and *Two Brothers and Their Baby Sister.* I also did two picture books for Coward-McCann, *The Wonder City* and *Washington Picture Book,* both being done to order. For Knopf, I did *Benny and His Penny.*

Then I began developing my historical books. I had no library facilities to draw upon, so the books I used for research had to be purchased by mail from secondhand dealers' catalogs, or borrowed, after I had made some visits there, from the Antiquarian Society Library at Worcester, Massachusetts. I soon began to find historical research a fascinating pursuit.

PHEBE FAIRCHILD, HER BOOK 1936 The Greenacres house was the inspiration for my first historical book, *Phebe Fairchild, Her Book.*

In Ohio where I was born and reared, there had been little to remind one of the past. It was unusual to see a house one hundred years old, because there were so few. But when I went to live in New England, I was conscious of history on all sides. Every town, every crossroads, every cemetery, every old house was filled with stories and traditions of the past which were still living, being handed down from one generation to the next. Many of the houses in Harwinton had been built in the 1700's and the Congregational Church in 1806. To live in New England was to become history-minded, the past lay so close behind the present. One could only understand the present by first delving into the past.

Our own house was built in 1790. From the very moment I first entered the door, I began to wonder about the life that had been lived there. When we opened up the huge old kitchen fireplace, we found the iron pot still hanging on a pot-hook on the crane, as if some bygone housewife of a century before had just gone away and left it there. I listened to stories told by my neighbors of their ancestors, the people who had built the town. I began to collect old children's books.

One of the first was a little book in green paper covers, called *Scenes in the Country*. The inscription on the flyleaf in faded ink, read:

> *"Kate Daniels Her Book October 1825*
> *From Her Cousins in Litchfield"*

Then the rhyme:

> "This is a preshious Book, indeed,
> Happy the Child who Loves to Read."

Although I did not realize it then, I was starting on a journey into childhood of the past.

I wanted to write a story of our house, to tell how the people lived in it in 1830, when it was just forty years old. What was family life like then? Village life, child life? I had to find out. I studied local town and church records; I visited historical societies and museums in the area. I studied old newspapers, letters, and diaries that had been preserved. I learned a great deal.

> "Children did not live lives of their own in those days; they lived in an adult world and were affected by everything that went on in that adult world. The very self-sufficiency of every farm, providing as it did everything necessary for living, in the way of shelter, food and clothing, gave the life of a child an inconspicuous place. Children were taught to be seen but not heard—the home was such a busy plant there wasn't time to listen to what the children had to say. Thrown early upon their own initiative, they developed inner resources of strength and vigor which enabled them to withstand the rigors of their harsh training and environment."*

* From "The Story of *Phebe Fairchild, Her Book*," by Lois Lenski. *Horn Book Magazine,* November 1937.

The early children's books in my collection which helped me particularly were: a little brown morocco-covered *Mother Goose;* a *Ladies' Pocket Library,* with gloomy black covers, full of rules for conduct and behavior; a pink paper-covered Watts' *Divine Songs for Children,* with the hymns which Phebe had to learn; a soiled and worn *Memoirs of Miriam Warner,* whose forlorn appearance in itself would give any child the heartache; and an eight-page book, *The Folly of Finery, or History of Mary Lawson,* which tells the sad fate of a little girl who loved pretty clothes and personal adornments. Last but not least was a tiny book, 1½ by 2½ inches, with only eight pages, which was simply bristling with eloquent objections to *Mother Goose,* as "silly rhymes, unfit for children to read." It was largely through this handful of little books that Phebe Fairchild came alive.

While I was writing *Phebe,* I lived in the year 1830. I did all the things the Fairchild family did, in imagination. I could see Aunt Hannah's loom in the weaving room upstairs and hear it thumping every day. I listened to the loud tick of the grandfather clock in the front hall, and wished the Fairchilds had left it there! I smelled the candles at candle-dipping time. I warmed myself at the great log fire in the kitchen fireplace. It didn't smoke for the Fairchilds, but it did for *us!*

It was like a living dream. The characters became so real, I talked about them to everybody. Stephen would ask me, "What did Phebe do today?" My typist, a neighbor girl, said, "The family is so large, the house won't hold them all." So she and I put the family to bed. We put the two little girls in the trundlebed in their parents' room. After Christopher, the traveling artist came and stayed, we sent Timothy up to Uncle Thad's to sleep, and then there was a bed for everybody! In fact, I talked about the Fairchilds so much that my husband said, "I think we'd better move out of the house and let the Fairchilds have it!"

After the book was published, I had frequent visits from teachers, librarians, and children. They all wanted to see the

North Parlor where Phebe put on Great-Aunt Pettifer's cape and bonnet, and the upstairs window out of which she jumped when she ran away. The house began to be known as the Fairchild house, and there was grave danger that the poor Balches who had built it would be forgotten. I was amused and a little alarmed to find out that I had created a legend! My visitors insisted that Phebe was a real person, despite all I could tell them to the contrary. Yes, Phebe was real, one librarian told me, so real, in fact, that she was buried in the Watertown Cemetery! Anybody could go and see her grave there. What better proof could I want? Of course Phebe was real. I was forced to admit that my brainchild had come to life.

Childhood of the Past In making a study of childhood of the past, clues are found in unexpected places.

One of the best sources is the old diaries. Not many children wrote them, but those who did were often very articulate. Here the child speaks in his own words across the gap of time from then to now. He gives us a vivid picture of his activities, especially of the large amount of work he did and the small amount of pleasure he enjoyed. Old letters, too, speak to us directly. From them, we hear the people talking, the exact expressions they used. In their own words, we sense the attitudes of adults to their children.

The old newspapers printed revealing advertisements, brief flashes into children's lives—children lost, stranded, or, unbelievably, left behind at some wayside stopping place by families traveling westward to Ohio. The parents seem to have expected some kind soul to pick the lost child up and bring him along—hence the advertisement—but often they were never heard from, had vanished entirely. Runaways were advertised—conditions must have been bad to make a child run away from home of parents or relatives. "Bound out" children were badly treated and often ran away. Even those children carefully nurtured in their own homes by loving parents, led difficult lives of repression and frustration, inhibited by strict and often cruel moral standards. Life was far from easy for many children in the early days of our country, and our hearts go out to them in sympathy when we read these undeniable clues to their misery.

There are other valuable sources of information.

Old account books show actual purchases made for the home or farm. They list "country pay"—farm produce exchanged for hard goods. Town and church records give amounts of money spent on bound-out children, or the price of an apron for a widow, who had been auctioned off by the town to the lowest bidder who would board and keep her, and work her very hard.

The best source of all is the early children's books. They throw a brilliant sidelight on every angle of the American child's life through the years, up to the present time. They reflect vividly the changing ideals of successive generations as clearly as our modern books for children reflect the ideals of the present age. From them we learn what adults thought of children, how they shaped their thinking, how they controlled their behavior and morals, how they dressed and fed them, disciplined, scolded, and punished them.

A careful study of all these available sources deflates any glorified, nostalgic ideas that we may have harbored about "the olden days." It tells us the plain truth, that childhood of the past was never easy, and many children were unable to survive its harshness and its difficulties. It is not surprising that the old cemeteries are filled with tiny headstones on children's graves, mute testimony to the hardships of their lives.

In writing my historical books, I wanted to describe the everyday life of people in a given period, to tell what they thought, felt, said, and did, how they got their food, shelter, and clothing, what their ideals were and how near they came to living up to them. I wanted to tell how their actions and beliefs grew out of their environment. In other words, I tried to give a lively picture of home life and village life as reflected in the life of the child.

During the course of my research, the past came alive for

me in a way it never did in the history books. I had hated history in school. To me it was only a meaningless procession of dates and battles to be memorized. But as soon as I really projected myself into the past, as soon as I looked at history from the point of view of the people who lived it, it became fascinating and absorbing and very much alive.

It was an engrossing task to get all the details correct. The characters must wear the right style of clothing, have the right kind of furniture in houses of the right architecture, built in the period described. Their manners, speech, and customs had to be exact. I learned not to have rugs on the floor in the days when all floors were sprinkled with sand. I learned to give my characters cornbread to eat and homespun clothing to wear, in the days before factories. I became steeped and saturated in all the outward appurtenances of a period, and in the inner feelings of the people as well. I practically donned a wig, took a pinch of snuff and acted in concert with my male hero. I put on the hooped skirts and bonnets of the little girls I wrote about. I loved all those details which made the past different from the present. But all the time, I knew in my heart that the child was no different, had still the same loves and hates, the same desires and frustrations, the same stoicism and courage, and the same joys and sorrows as the child living today.

By thus living the past in imagination, I tried to make the child of yesterday as understandable as the child of today. My explorations into the lives of past-and-gone children taught me, as nothing else could, the eternal truth of childhood.

In historical books, there is a great deal of work that goes on behind the scenes, which the reader never suspects.

For *Phebe Fairchild, Her Book,* I made a complete genealogy of three generations of the Fairchild family. I found an actual stagecoach timetable, listing the stops and inns from New Haven to Winton in the 1830's, and I was able to pick out a stage for Phebe to take, when she traveled to her grandmother's in the country. For *A-Going to the Westward,* using the 1811 calendar, map, and almanac, I made a chart of the exact number of miles Betsy's family traveled each day; I knew where each river and every tavern was located, and exactly where the Bartletts were on each day of the long journey.

Such details must be carefully worked out before an outline of the story can be made. Such an outline will show exactly what is to happen in each chapter before I begin to write. It is not easy to think a plot through to conclusion in advance of the writing. But if and when it is done, it allows an author to write with greater selectivity and stricter economy of words.

A-GOING TO THE WESTWARD 1937   A Connecticut neighbor loaned me a box of old letters that had been in her family for over a hundred years. It was one of them that got me very excited. In the early 1800's a Connecticut boy wrote to his cousin in New Connecticut (Ohio) saying: "There are a great many people a-going to the Westward."

This letter gave me the title for my book and spurred me on to a study of eyewitness accounts left by travelers, describing their experiences en route. This was the peak of the period of westward migration when Ohio was the frontier, and the word "Ohio" was on everyone's lips. In many Connecticut towns, more than half the population packed their household goods into covered wagons and followed the dusty white roads leading westward. In 1811, it took from four to six weeks to make the journey, because of bad roads, overturned wagons, dangers of fording streams, shortage of food supplies, and many other risks and dangers. But neither the dangers nor deliberate propaganda were able to stop the steady procession of emigrants. Cheap land, good black soil with no stones and no hills, corn twelve feet high—these were the attractions. In my book, I took the Bartlett family to the Westward, trying always to see their exciting and dangerous experiences through the eyes of a child, my heroine, Betsy Bartlett.

BOUND GIRL OF COBBLE HILL 1938   A quarter of a mile from Greenacres, in Harwinton, Connecticut, at the corner of the old Hartford Turnpike, there stands a fine old Revolutionary homestead. Local tradition says that it was originally an inn, and that George Washington and the French leader, Rochambeau, once stopped there, and were waited upon by a local townsgirl. Seven miles away, in Litchfield, another old homestead has been restored as a colonial inn with many local traditions. These associations stimulated the writing of a story of a young girl who might have been living at such an inn.

Bound Girl of Cobble Hill was the result. Mindwell Gibbs' father was lost in the Revolutionary War. In accordance with local Connecticut custom, she was indentured or "bound out" to her uncle, the landlord of a busy inn "on the great road from Hartford to New York," in 1789, the year of Washington's inauguration.

In return for "board, lodging, schooling, apparel and physic," Mindwell Gibbs was obliged to serve tavern guests from dawn to dark, learn to spin and weave and "mind her manners" strictly. In the story, Mindwell does her best to "mind well," but difficulties arise and her course does not always run smoothly. In the end, however, she makes a place of her own, not only in her uncle's home, but in the life of the town. My background material for the binding out of orphan children was obtained in the New Haven Historical Society library, where I examined more than a hundred indenture papers dated from 1740 to 1840 and studied many letters and expense accounts relating to the care of such children. This was considered the best way of caring for orphans before the days of orphanages.

Mindwell's lot as a bound girl was not an easy one. Life was hard in those days, even for children in their own homes, and only the fittest survived. Weak children pined away and died. Strong ones gained in strength and grew to manhood and womanhood. This may account for the inherent ruggedness of the New England character.

OCEAN-BORN MARY 1939   It was a Vermont friend who wrote me one day, saying, "Have you ever heard the legend of

Ocean-Born Mary?" She did not say what it was. I stared at that piece of paper. "Ocean-Born Mary!" I said aloud. "What a wonderful title for a girl's book!"

She was a real person, of course. I lost no time in looking up all I could find out about her, about her birth on the ocean, the rescue by the pirate and the pirate's gift of the green silk brocade. I learned about the house in Henniker, New Hampshire, where she spent the latter part of her life and which now bears her name. I went to Henniker for a visit.

I heard all the fantastic tales that had grown up around Mary, although she had been dead over 130 years. I decided that if the pirate *did* enter her later life and *did* build the Henniker house with his gold, something must have happened in between. So I set out to supply the missing link. In my book, Mary is visiting her aunt in Portsmouth in 1730, when she is twelve. The pirate comes to this seaport and learns that Mary is the child whose life he saved. Mary learns that he is the man who saved her life and, although he is a desperate, wicked outlaw, Mary is able to do him a kindness and win his gratitude.

The background of this story tells of the New Hampshire mast industry and the beginnings of revolt against the mother country, which led to the Revolutionary War. In my research I learned that certain large trees in the forests were reserved for the King's Navy and could not be felled. These trees were marked with the *Broad Arrow*. What was the broad arrow, what did it look like, I wondered. Endless research threw no light on the subject, various librarians versed in historical lore were consulted, but no one knew.

One day I was in New York, browsing in the secondhand bookshops along 59th Street, where sidewalk tables were overflowing with shabby books of all kinds, priced at five and ten cents each. I opened one of them and stared. I could hardly believe it. There before my eyes was the Broad Arrow! It was pictured in a book where I might have least expected it: *Travels at Home* by Edward Everett Hale. A good example of the thrills of historical research!

INDIAN CAPTIVE 1941   Three years of serious study went into the making of this book, with help from various Seneca Indian authorities. When I learned that the Seneca Indians had never before been correctly illustrated, I felt I had the opportunity to make a real contribution, and this was an incentive to make the illustrations as authentic as the text. That in the end, the book earned the approval of Dr. Arthur C. Parker, himself a Seneca Indian, was a great satisfaction to me.

At this time, I learned of a privately printed book dealing with reminiscences of family life in western New York State, prior to 1815, which mentioned "the Indian captive Molly Jemison." I inferred from this that she had been commonly known by her nickname, Molly, so I called her Molly in my story. Her story is well known, for when she was an old woman, she told it to a visitor and it was printed. Captured by the Senecas in eastern Pennsylvania in 1758, she was taken by them to Pittsburgh, then to Ohio, and later to the Genesee River Valley, where she lived with them till the end of her long life. The remarkable thing about her experience is that she had a number of opportunities to return to the whites, but refused them all.

My book deals with the first two years of her captivity. It tells of her capture, her first rebellion and despair and of her hope of escape. Then of her gradual awakening to the true wisdom and kindness of the Indians and of her final unwillingness to leave them.

This story presents two contrasting pictures of child life of the past, that of the Seneca Indians and that of the early settlers. The fact that a white child captive so often refused to return to the whites, but preferred to stay with the Indians, gives cause for wonder. This was not an isolated case. It happened not once, but over and over, at different periods and in different localities. Why? We can only conclude that Mary Jemison and other white children were happier and more contented than they had been in their own homes, and that the Indian way of life made a strong appeal.

The long months of study which were required for this book, took their toll of my strength. After the illustrations were completed in pencil, I wrote to my publishers to tell them it would be impossible for me to ink them in, as I had done in preceding books, for an indefinite period. Delay would have meant holding the book over for another year, and this the publishers were reluctant to do. After the printer offered to reproduce the pencil drawings just as they were, by a high-light halftone offset process, the book went through as scheduled, and became one of the most beautiful I had ever done.

PURITAN ADVENTURE 1944   For *Puritan Adventure,* the primary sources were many, for child life in both old "Merry" England and in Puritanical New England, showing the contrast between the two.

There were many restrictions placed on children by the Puritans. Children were allowed no fairy tales, idle songs, or nursery rhymes. They could not indulge in idleness; while sitting to rest, a girl must knit; while tending sheep or cattle, children should spin with a distaff or knot or weave tape. They carried water and wood, they scoured pewter, they scrubbed floors. Running, laughing, babbling, cackling, playing, jumping, hollering—all these were wrong and evil. Children were to labor constantly, to be obedient to parents and all those in authority, and to guard against pride and vainglory. Idleness was the worst sin of all. They lived constantly in fear of reproof, admonition, and punishment, not only from their parents but from tithing-man, constable, and magistrate.

This was the most difficult book I ever attempted to write. I suffered so because all normal instincts of the Puritan children were so restricted and repressed. The evidence is in black and white, in hundreds of sources, and one cannot fail to see it. In my story, I solved the difficulty by creating a fictional character, Aunt Charity, a new arrival from old England, who remained a human being in all her dealings with her sister's children. She brought them their first Christmas celebration, in imitation of Old England, and was duly reproved for it.

The harsh treatment of Puritan children had a lasting influence, and was but the forerunner of continued childhood repression carried on through the eighteenth and nineteenth centuries in this country, and which only began to relax by the twentieth.

BLUEBERRY CORNERS 1940   *Blueberry Corners* is the story of an easier period, the 1840's in Connecticut. In it I used a lot of local historical material. I told of the coming of the first train into the Naugatuck River Valley, repeating a tale told to me by a ninety-five-year-old woman who remembered it vividly. I told how the first circus came to town and what a dreadful thing some people thought it was, for Puritanism still lingered. I told how big the blueberries grew on the hills and in the swamps, and how "Aunty Ruth" gave a tree of apples to the school children and got her name in the town history for doing so. I was able to tell of a parentless Thanksgiving and the visit of a Yankee peddler with treasures in his pack; and how the arrival of an Episcopal family with strange ideas of celebrating Christmas, gave a little girl the idea of bringing Christmas for the first time into the strict Congregational parson's home.

I imagined the setting as Harwinton, Connecticut, "where the biggest blueberries grew in 1940, just as they did a hundred years before, in 1840"—thus reads the dedication.

It is a happy book, for while many of the Puritanical repressions were still being practiced, children in some ways were able to lead more normal and natural lives and to occasionally assert themselves. It would be a long time, though —another hundred years—before they began to "rule the roost" and have things entirely their own way.

My Picture Books   The 1930's saw the beginnings of both my historical books and my picture books. *Phebe Fairchild,*

Her Book was published in 1936, followed by five others by 1940, and two thereafter. *Sugarplum House* and *Gooseberry Garden,* two beautiful picture books, were published by Harper's in 1934 and 1935. The Mr. Small series began with *The Little Auto* in 1934, followed by *Sailboat, Airplane* and *Train* by 1940. The Davy books were begun in 1943. So this was a prolific decade.

The historical books were long serious undertakings, which sometimes bogged me down; so, concurrent with them, for my own pleasure, I made picture books because they were such fun to do. Stokes did not publish picture books and gave me permission to go elsewhere, so I found another publisher—Oxford—for them.

The making of a picture book is always sheer pleasure to me. I have always had a special place in my heart for the youngest children. As early as 1934, I wrote:

> "I enjoy my work for the youngest children, because I feel I understand them best and sense their point of view. I love the freshness of their unspoiled outlook upon the world, their wholehearted acceptance of life, their lack of self-consciousness, their instinctive humor. I love the ease with which they travel from the world of reality about them to the gay, fantastic world of imagination and humor, accepting both, but not confusing one with the other."

Every artist likes to draw pictures, and when he draws people, he likes to draw them doing things—walking, running, playing, eating, fighting—in all sorts of actions. The next step is to make a succession of pictures, showing successive actions which tell a story. This is the oldest way of telling a story and has been used from the days of the caveman's pictographs on down to the comic strip of today.

The young child who cannot read words, *can* read pictures. He can, in fact, draw pictures of his own and other people's activities, several years before his conscious mind can be taught to read printed words. So his understanding of pictures comes very early, often before the age of one year. In the preschool years, he looks at the picture of a child in action and understands what he is doing. As he looks at a series of pictures of successive actions, the whole story unfolds—he needs no words. Each picture is an exciting experience, a happening in itself. The thought stimulated by one picture carries over into the next. He loves to turn the pages.

This is why the picture book came into being. In it the pictures are the important thing. If words are also used, they merely reinforce the pictures. Often, when the words are not right, the child will disregard them, look at the pictures and make up his own story.

How can an artist get words and pictures right? In only one way—by trying them out on the child and getting his reactions.

When Stephen was small, I made pictures for him and he made pictures for me. He began to draw at the age of one and a half, as soon as he could hold a pencil. His father and his mother drew pictures all day long—why shouldn't he? Drawing was as much a part of his life as eating and sleeping, and as necessary for his well-being. He had from the beginning a sure and fearless touch. He was never afraid, he could draw anything. It was natural that I should draw pictures for him, not to show him how to do it, for he never needed to be shown. But I drew pictures for him that would tell a story and could be made into a book.

A picture book for the very young is not a casual thing, dreamed up in a moment. Only constant association with a child makes it possible. It is not easy to think as a child thinks, because our adult minds are too cluttered with nonessentials, too overloaded with preconceived ideas. The idea must be expressed in not too many words, keeping everything irrelevant out. There must be details, but only those that are important to the child. Every line of each drawing has to mean something. Meaningless lines must be omitted. This is why photographs do not serve the same purpose, for they are too inclusive. Every word of the text must be carefully chosen. I work the drawings and the text together, back and forth. Sometimes I make a change in the drawings to fit the text. Sometimes I change the text to fit the drawing. The first rough drawings are made in a "dummy," a simulated book, with text and drawings in pencil, so they can be quickly and easily changed.

A picture book goes through a long process of change and growth before it reaches completion. I make a dummy and I think it is just right, at least it satisfies the adult me. But is it right for the child? Will it be understandable and meaning-ful to the three- or four-year-old? Does it touch his life? Will it reach him? After many years of experience, I feel I ought to know the requirements for a particular age. But I dare not trust my own judgment, so I take it to children.

Where do I get my ideas?

Always from the child himself, from one child or a group. Sometimes from a chance remark or a specific happening or a universal experience. It is not something merely amusing or cute. Somehow, I must catch the essence of the child's life in the simple idea presented.

For example, *Davy's Day* is the real Davy's actual experi-ence in a single day. The other Davy books present his further growing experiences. *Mr. and Mrs. Noah* grew out of Davy's play with a toy Noah's Ark set.

I once heard a little girl say to another, "Let's play house." Those three words suggested the title for a picture book. Playing house is a universal experience of little girls. They re-enact the activities of mother and children in their own homes. I had no little girl of my own to watch and observe, so I had to borrow some. I went to a school and talked to the kindergarten children. In a play-house corner, I watched and listened to little girls cooking, washing and ironing, sweeping, etc. A friend who had two little girls took down notes of their play-conversation for me. The result was my book, *Let's Play House* (1944).

Books that have their roots in the child's own life never fail to satisfy him. It is most important to put the book to the test of the sharp eye and keen, open mind of the child for whom it is intended. I have always found children's ideas, questions, and criticisms clear, concrete, helpful, and more than that, tremendously inspiring. This step, consultation, is the most important of all, for it means adapting the book to the child's need and understanding. I would not miss this contact, this rapport with the living child, for anything.

When a book is just right, the young child immediately *lives* it. After hearing *The Little Train* read aloud for the first time, Davy put on overalls and cap, found an empty tin can for an oil can, and an old rag, and WAS Engineer Small. After hearing *The Little Sailboat,* Mrs. Duff's small son would "collect a small basket, a toy dog, a walking stick for a fishing-rod, and go happily sailing away in an arm-chair to perform with scrupulous exactness and complete satisfaction all the little doings of Captain Small's day." In both cases, the identification was immediate and complete.

The *Read-and-Sing Books* came about naturally. I happened to be showing a picture book to Davy at four, who could not read. The book, *The Little Farm,* had been read to him frequently and he knew the text by heart. He just began out of his own sheer joy in the book to sing it, all the way through, to a little tune he made up as he went along. He kept turning the pages, looking at each picture and singing the entire text until he reached the end. I listened in amazement.

That gave me an idea. Why can't children learn to sing their books as well as read them? I remembered all the controversy about "why Johnny cannot read," and the thought crossed my mind that maybe if he could sing his book—the words in the book—it might help him to learn to read the words. Singing the words would be pure joy and not hard work. That was the start of the little series of *Read-and-Sing Books* for which Clyde Robert Bulla made the lovely tunes. The titles are: *I Went for a Walk, At Our House,* and *When I Grow Up.*

The Mr. Small Books I could not possibly have created Mr. Small, had it not been for my small son. Automobiles were Stephen's major interest, with other vehicles secondary—the train, the tractor, the airplane, the fire engine, the sailboat. His interest in these was not passive, but active. He wanted to know *what made the vehicle go.*

I watched Stephen and his little friends play by the hour. It was imaginary play, they imagined that the wagon or kiddie car or tricycle was an automobile or a train. If they had small cars, they pushed them with their hands to make them go, and they made all the noises that an automobile makes. They *never* personified an automobile or a train. They never imagined a face on the front, they never made it talk like a person or run away, or move of its own volition. Always the boy identified himself *not* with the vehicle, but with the driver of the car, the engineer of the train, the pilot of the airplane, etc.

For years we have had books in which trains are personified, carry on conversations and frequently, or usually, run away. This is the imagination of adults, not of children. It has been done so often, it has become stereotyped.

In the Mr. Small books, the reader identifies himself with the driver, the engineer, the pilot, the farmer, the captain, the fireman, the cowboy, and the father. He *becomes* Mr. Small and enjoys his experiences vicariously. These books have held a never-ending fascination for two generations of boy and girl readers alike, making a dramatic appeal which belies their very simplicity. There is a some unseen bond between the child and Mr. Small, which I myself cannot explain. Children in foreign countries, even those still undeveloped and unacquainted with American customs, have been captivated by the appeal of Mr. Small and his doings, as is evidenced by the many foreign editions of the books.

The Little Auto was the first in the series. One of the first words that Stephen ever spoke was "auto," hence the title. Because he was four at the time I was making the book, I drew the main character in the proportions of a four-year-old, but I called him Mr. Small, because Stephen always played he was a *man*. The book shows Mr. Small, Stephen in disguise, doing all the things to the little auto that Stephen had seen his daddy do to our family car—pumping up tires, putting oil in, pouring water in the radiator . . . and then going for a ride, and getting gas in town. I told the story with the fewest possible words and illustrated it with the simplest possible drawings. I was allowed only one color, besides the key plate, which was black and gray wash; and the book first sold for 75¢.

The book was rejected by an eminent but shortsighted editor, who hastily glanced through my dummy and handed it back to me, saying: "There is no story." At the Oxford University Press, the editor, Grace Hogarth, accepted it. She told me afterwards that she was very daring to take it. Fairies were the style in the 1930's, so a book about an automobile was an innovation and a great risk! Sales for the first year or two seemed to bear this out. The book made not a ripple. Nobody noticed.

It was a little ahead of its time. It took a few years for it to catch up. By the time one generation of boys had gotten their hands on it, refusing to let it go, copies were selling by the thousands. It was "no story" to an editor, but sheer drama to thousands of boys and girls. In 1956, Mr. Small celebrated his twenty-fifth birthday, with appropriate celebrations. The book was now a "best seller." It had come into its own. The second, and now soon, a third generation of children has loved and enjoyed the Mr. Small books. As Frederic Melcher said, "Mr. Small has become an American institution!"

One day when Stephen was three, we were walking out in the field behind our house and we happened to see an airplane fly over. Airplanes were not common in our area in the early 1930's, so the sight was unusual. I said to Stephen, "Let's wave to the man up there!"

Stephen looked at me in surprise. "Is there a man up there?" he asked.

Before this, I suppose, an airplane was just another bird

flying overhead to him, a bird with a different name. So I made it a point in my book, *The Little Airplane,* to show views of the airplane sitting on the ground, with cab door open, and the pilot climbing in and stepping out.

Another question came from Stephen: "What does he do to make it go?"

This was a hard question to answer, because I had to first find out myself. I had never flown at this time, and had never been inside an airplane. Even if I had, it would not have helped me with my problem, but by being persistent, I soon found the help I needed. I went to a small private airport in Litchfield, where two young Italian boys had a Piper Cub and were taking passengers up for short rides on Sunday afternoons. One of them sensed exactly what I wanted. He sat down on the running board of our car beside me and talked in four-year-old words that I could understand. He said, "You have a stick—a joy-stick, and when you push it this way, it does so-and-so . . ." He told me the whole process in simple words and I understood them. Then I wrote the book. Children seem to understand it, too, for they love to read it.

Why did I use a simple Piper Cub for my airplane, a steam engine for my train, and a simple car for my automobile? Why be old-fashioned, why not be up-to-date, why should not these vehicles be modernized—a jet plane, a diesel engine, an automatic Cadillac? These questions are often asked me. The simple model best tells the story in its basic essence, which the child, even the very young child, can comprehend.

The Little Farm brought no difficulties. In fact it came to life right on my own doorstep, and I would have had to be blind not to see and experience it. The hay in the field on all sides of my studio was being cut in the summer of 1941 by a young farmer neighbor, who had just purchased a brand-new tractor, shiny green and beautiful. He was flattered to demonstrate it and explain every detail of its operations in cutting hay, hauling apples, and all the routine jobs on the farm. So Mr. Small turned farmer quite easily.

Several years later, the book was Davy's favorite in the summers he spent at Greenacres. The book came to life each day right before his eyes, for the same young farmer was using the tractor to cut our hay. Having a ride on Mr. Small's tractor was the epitome of adventure, one to be repeated each summer as he grew older.

Stephen took an active and proprietary interest in the Mr. Small books as they were being made, supervising every detail of word and picture. By the time I made the Train book, he was ten. He had never been inside the cab of a steam engine, nor had I, so together we had a great adventure. We rode in the cab of a train from Torrington to Winsted, Connecticut, as guests of the engineer. In Winsted, at the end of the line, the engine waited several hours before returning, and there I had plenty of time to ask questions of the engineer and to make sketches of the cab interior. Many details of text and pictures were later worked out with the enthusiastic cooperation of a class of five-year-olds at Horace Mann School in New York, all of whom knew far more about trains than I did!

I shall always treasure a letter which they wrote me after the book was published—to their complete satisfaction. I have often had suggestions for new things for Mr. Small to do, but this was a wholesale order:

Horace Mann School
Dec. 9, 1940

"Dear Miss Lenski:

We enjoyed helping you with the Train book. We hope you will write some more. We wish you would make one about Mr. Small being Santa Claus. Let Mr. Small be a fireman sometime. Make him be:

a life-saver
a policeman
a milkman
a street car conductor
a bus driver
a subway engineer

169

a butcher
a mail man
a door man
a tailor
or an elevator man
in some of your books.
We hope we will see you soon.
Please, will you come again?
Good-bye, Miss Lenski"

One thing is very sure. I will *never* run out of ideas as long as I have friends among children!

The Davy Books In the summers of 1943–4–5, I had the great pleasure of having Davy (David Chisholm) with me at Greenacres. In 1944, he stayed eight months. Margaret, his mother, was ill and unable to care for him. By this time I was better able to assess and objectively observe the reactions of a small boy's growth and development, than I was when younger, with Laird or Stephen. All my experiences with Davy enriched my understanding of childhood. How fortunate I was to have him for three summers. But the first few weeks were not easy.

Davy at three was a very sad and pitiful little boy, who had been badly handled by various housekeepers. Shy and timid by nature, when he first came to me, he held his head down frowning, and refused to look up or say a word. He distrusted the whole world. He had no faith in anyone except his daddy, who brought him to me and left him. He was bitterly homesick and cried for days and days. He did not know that he had come into an atmosphere of kindness.

I tried everything. I talked to him to try to divert him. I played with his toys, I told stories, I sang songs, I made castles in the sand. Each day I did these things over and over, but nothing helped—his heart was broken. I had never seen such grief displayed by a child so young for so long a time. He would not listen or play. He did not want to be cuddled on my lap. He cried and cried, day after day. Each night he cried himself to sleep. At the house, he refused to eat. Only the milk he drank sustained him.

It was enough to break a stouter heart than mine. I did not know what to do or where to turn. Kindness made no impression on him. I exhausted all my resources and was about to give up. But what would become of him if I did? I could not give up and I was in despair because I could not reach him. I cried as much as he did, and could not sleep at night. I must win him somehow, I must keep on trying. . . .

Then suddenly, the unexpected happened. One morning Davy ate his cereal for breakfast without any urging. He looked up at me and smiled. "Let's go to the sandpile, Lo-lo," he said. He put the toys in his basket voluntarily and carried it to the sandpile himself. The battle was over. That day he did not cry or any day thereafter. He played happily with his toys in the sand. He talked to me and told me what he was making. From that time on, he was a different boy. He began to blossom out like a wilted flower after the rain.

Whatever I did, Davy did, whether cooking in the kitchen, weeding in the garden, or playing in or near my studio while I was working. Whenever I wanted him to take a nap, I would lie down on the couch beside him, and he would say to me, "Put head on pillow, Lo-lo. Good-night, Lo-lo."

I had made the first Davy book, *Davy's Day,* before he came, and when I received the color proofs, I showed them to him. A photograph shows him sitting on my lap expressing his delight in the pictures, a beaming smile on his face, pointing out details with his finger. Why wouldn't he love it? It was a recreation of his own life in every detail. There he saw it on the printed page. But he had some reservations. One picture shows a bed cut off by the spine of the book. For days, Davy hunted for the other half of the bed, turning the pages over and over. Alas! he never found it! Had I had this reaction before publication, I would have drawn the entire bed. I learned a valuable lesson—a half-bed does not convey the idea of a whole bed to a child.

By the next summer, Davy was more mature, happier, and more responsive, and we had eight delightful months together. He chattered freely and happily, making many unique and startling observations about everything around him. He was very musical, loved to sing, and often sang his comments to tunes made up by himself. Everything he did suggested a book. Because it poured rain all the second summer, he and I played *Mr. and Mrs. Noah* in my studio. He had a set of Noah toys carved out of wood by his grandfather, also a large wooden ark. He gave me my orders to make a book of that title, and supervised every step of the making. He sat on a high stool beside me as I colored the dummy. "Paint the rain blue, Lo-lo!" he cried. So I painted the rain blue. I took down in notebooks hundreds of his poetic sayings. Once when I was resting beside him, he said, "Do you even write when you are taking a nap, Lo-lo?"

By the time the third summer was over, I had made notes or dummies for six picture books, all inspired by his companionship. My experiences with Davy were some of the richest I have ever had with any child. I treasure the memory of them.

THE FORTIES *and* FIFTIES

PERSONAL 1940'S AND 1950'S

The Vicissitudes of Winter The summers in Connecticut were delightful (except when it rained continuously) but oh! the winters! I had not lived there many years before I came to realize how tough and rugged my New England neighbors were. They had to be tough, like their ancestors before them, in order to survive. Each year I dreaded the approach of winter. Perhaps it was because I love summer, the growing season, so much that I hated to see autumn and even beautiful "Indian summer" with its falling leaves come. It gave me a desolate feeling to know that the long period of dark, sunless, and often bitterly cold days lay ahead.

Through the fourteen years that I spent in Connecticut, from 1929 to 1943, most of the winters were very cold. One winter, in 1934, the temperature went to 40 degrees below, and we had to throw all the furnace heat into one room and supplement this with a huge fire of burning logs in the fireplace, to keep even reasonably warm. Many winters, it went to 20 degrees below, and always each year as low as to 10 degrees below. In addition to low temperatures, there were frequent winter gales, blizzards and ice storms, plus deep, deep snows. I have photographs that show snowdrifts as high as our second-story windows. The coldest nights and hardest freezes always came, ironically, on the most beautiful full-moon nights. I can remember standing in my south bedroom upstairs, looking out the window and seeing the full moon in all its glory throwing long shadows of the great elm tree across the icy glaze of the snow-covered field. I can still hear the whistling of the winter wind down the great chimney of our old house and seeing nothing but a blur of falling snow outside each window, as if the snow were coming from all directions at once. I can recall lying in bed under heaps of blankets, listening to the harsh cracking of tree limbs in an ice storm, each crack as loud and sharp as the explosion of a shotgun. The branches, ice-covered, became heavy-laden and when the winds blew, they cracked and broke, falling to the ground. Tree trunks as large as a foot in diameter often broke and fell. Each storm meant a big clean-up job afterwards.

Beautiful? Yes. Often the sight was heart-breakingly beautiful, with the sun or the full moon shining on each of the multitudinous tiny fingerlike branches, the whole shining like fairyland. But I could not enjoy the beauty. . . . We had had cold winters in Ohio when I was young, and I had been accustomed to them. We lived through them without central heating and other modern conveniences and with no noticeable ill effects. I already knew them by experience, but these in Connecticut on top of our high hill, a thousand feet in elevation, were much harder for me.

I was never warm all winter. Even in a room heated to 80 degrees and uncomfortable for the rest of the family, I was always shivering. I became very susceptible to sore throat, and each winter barely escaped pneumonia. Our electricity was erratic. At the approach of the slightest storm, it always went off. This meant the electric pump stopped pumping, and we had to pump water by hand from the cistern and carry it in by the pailful. The current often stayed off for as long as two weeks at a time, and this meant the use of kerosene lamps and candles. Romantic? Yes. Beautiful? Yes. But fourteen winters of it was enough.

My family were more rugged than I and gloried in the joys of winter. It was always a joke to them that I disliked winter so much. My husband teased me unmercifully when I did my little seasonal picture book, called *I Like Winter!* (1950). "You know how you hate winter, and here you go, deceiving all the innocent little children in the country by telling them you *like* it!" I tried to protest: "It is not *I* who like it, my child reader likes it, loves it! *Every* child *loves* winter, even those in the south who have never seen snow or experienced it at all!" But still they poked fun at me.

When I was making my plans to go to South Dakota to get material for *Prairie School,* in the spring of 1950, the teacher, Ruth Carter, kept writing me: "Still cold here! Don't come yet!" I wrote to the children, "When it goes *down* to 40°, it is *winter* here in Florida." They wrote back to me, "When it goes *up* to 40° here in South Dakota, we call it *spring!*" I waited and waited for it to warm up in South Dakota. But at last I had to go, in order to visit the school before the end of the school year. It was still too soon for my comfort. My arrival caused a horrible blizzard and kept me marooned for five days in town. On my first trip of nine miles out to the rural school, I rode with a farmer in a jeep in a second blizzard, with only a flapping curtain between me and the elements, my hands so cold I could not hold a pencil. When the driver came to a deep arroyo, and got out to steady two planks across the bottomless abyss, and to see that his front wheels were properly aligned, so we could pass over without landing in a heap at the bottom, my heart was pounding and I was shaking from head to foot. As we passed over— safely—I held my breath and told myself I was a perfect idiot. When I finally saw through the blur of whirling snowflakes, a row of windows on what might be a schoolhouse beside the jeep, I told myself what a fool I was—to do all this just to write a story!

The real climax of our cold Connecticut winters came on December 26, 1947, the date of the big New York blizzard —which dropped twenty-six inches of snow in forty-five minutes—the only storm which ever competed with the famous legendary blizzard of 1888. Of course, that *would* be the very date we chose well in advance unknowingly, to make our departure to Florida. On the previous day, it began to snow and to snow hard. But our train reservations were bought for the next day, and all arrangements made with plumber and furnace man for disconnecting heat, pump, water, lights, etc., for closing the house for the winter. So plans could not be changed. Our train was to leave New York at midday on the 27th, and we planned to take the early seven-o'clock train from Torrington to New York that morning, as it made a nice connection.

At noon the day before, Elizabeth Riley, one of my editor friends, telephoned me from New Canaan, where she was visiting. "Oh, Lois," she said, "get to New York today if you possibly can. You'll never be able to get there if you wait until tomorrow." She told me the storm was going to get much worse, and we should leave the house at once and go. She told me to go to her apartment on Thirtieth Street and to get the key from the superintendent and sleep there—if Stephen and Mr. Covey could go to his club.

There was only one train for the rest of that day, late in the evening, so we rushed to get ready. Mr. Covey and Stephen put the trunks in the car early in the afternoon to drive them to Torrington and check them. Then they were to come back (six miles) and pick me up. We would go to town and have dinner at the hotel before taking the evening train. It sounded like an easy way out of a perilous situation. I finished all the last-minute details and waited. The furnace had been turned off and the house began to get cold. No food was left in the icebox. I waited and waited—they did not come. Outside the windows, a howling storm was raging, and the wind was whistling down the chimney. The storm had grown much worse since they left. I made myself try to rest. I stretched out on the couch and covered myself with my heavy winter coat, as the blankets were all packed away. The house got colder and so did I. I could not rest, I could only see the raging snow flying past the windows, shutting out all land-marks . . . and still they did not come. I knew now they must be stuck somewhere. It should not take four hours to go six miles and back. I lay on the couch, sick with fear and worry. . . .

It was nearly dark when they got back, with a tale to tell of broken chains, snowdrifts, and unplowed roads. But they had stopped at the local garage and brought the garage man along, to drive us to town and to bring our car back to his place, later to store it in our garage. We left as quickly as we could. To keep my hat from sailing off in the gale, I put it in a paper sack, tied a wool scarf over my head, and clutching purse, paper sack, and overnight bag under my arms, waded the knee-high snow to get to the car out in the road. The town plow had come by and thrown up piles of snow six feet high beside the road, closing our driveway. We rode in grim silence, slipping from one side of the slippery, rutty road to the other, but I felt confidence in the strong arm of the tough German driver at the wheel and knew he would get us there. Once Stephen poked me and grinned, saying: "How's this for an adventure, Mother?" I was able to smile back.

The town of Torrington was deserted, with snow-covered, stalled cars standing around in unexpected places. Not a soul was in sight. The hotel was deserted, too, except for the three hardy Covey wayfarers. The good meal which we ate leisurely, helped to revive our spirits. We were well-fed, and best of all, warm, and we felt our troubles were over. All we had to do now was to get on the train for New York. We waited what seemed hours at the hotel, until such time as our expected train might come. When we got to the station, it was filled with people, waiting like us for the New York train. The station was cold and got colder. We sat and shivered. At last a train came, and with sighs of relief, we embarked.

The train could actually go, too, and eventually to our surprise, landed us at Bridgeport and dumped us. Another long wait in the icy wind, and we clambered on an express train that suddenly appeared out of the snowy void on its way down from Hartford or Boston or somewhere. At any rate it was headed for New York, our ultimate goal. It was now about 11:30 P.M. The coach was one of the then new and fancy ones with wide stretches of picture windows on both sides, to give riders the illusion of sailing right through the raging blizzard. There were no shades to pull, so to shut out the sight, we had to close our eyes. There were few passengers, most people had the good sense not to venture out. We curled up as best we could on separate seats, and wrapped our heavy coats around us to try to keep warm. The heat went off if it had ever been on, the train got colder and colder, and it went slower and slower. As it approached New York, it seemed to do so with great reluctance, as if leery of conditions it might meet there, and rightly. In the suburbs it began to barely crawl . . . it crawled and crept inch by inch . . . would it stop or could it keep going? Was it breathing its last? Inch by inch we moved . . . and hooray! we made it, without having to get out and push!

We unwrapped our cramped and frozen nether extremities and tried to see if we could walk again.

We came into the main lobby at Grand Central Station at 2 A.M., and what a sight met our eyes! People, hundreds of stranded people lying on the marble floor, heads on suitcases and luggage, sleeping or hoping to. They were so close together, it was hard to find a path without treading on somebody's fingers or toes. We crossed over to a subway exit and held a conference. Then Mr. Covey and Stephen went at once down the subway—no snow there, so it was still running

—and rode to Fourteenth Street, to go to the Salmagundi Club where comfortable beds awaited them.

I could not go to my editor's apartment at 2 A.M., and I did not like the idea of sleeping on the marble floor in the station. So I went into the Waldorf Hotel adjoining. I knew it was useless to ask for a room, but I got in line with some other hopeful souls and did it. "Sorry, Madam, no rooms are vacant," said the clerk politely. "But you are welcome to sleep in the lobby if you can find a chair." Most of the chairs were filled, but I found the last empty one and sat down—with relief. No snow here either. And it was warm, so I got thawed out. But I could not sleep sitting upright in a straight-backed chair. I watched the other people, all kinds in all positions, sleeping here, there, and everywhere. Soon two women, who had been sitting on a couch near me, got up and vanished. Quickly I slid over to the couch and lay down on it full length, using my coat for a blanket. I tried to relax and sleep, but it was difficult. I may have dozed a little, but it seemed no time at all before a bellboy tapped me gently on the shoulder and said, "Sorry, madam, it's seven o'clock. No more sleeping in the lobby."

I got up, tried to open my eyes and brush my clothes up a bit. I then found my way to the subway entrance, took a train to Thirty-fourth Street, and walked from there to my friend's apartment.

I shall never forget the sight of Fifth Avenue. It was like a snowbound lane in the country. Nothing moving, stalled cars and trucks almost hidden under great mounds of snow were standing abandoned. Great mounds of snow shoveled up the day before were now covered by fresh snow, as clean and unspoiled as snow in the country. Only one or two other people were abroad besides myself, making footprints in the narrow footpath on what had been sidewalks. But the strangest part of it all was the silence, the ghastly silence, as if all life in the city and its raucous noises had ended forever, and only the elements, the hard wicked hand of winter, had taken over.

I roused the superintendent, who let me into my friend's

apartment. Here again, blessed relief. No snow inside and pleasant warmth for a welcome. I have no memory of eating anything, although I knew the icebox was full. I could not get to bed fast enough, and this time I slept.

Mr. Covey phoned and again, by subway, we managed to get to Pennsylvania Station, check our bags, have lunch, and catch our train leisurely. Stephen left us here, after "our big adventure," taking a local train to Philadelphia to return to his school. Once more, blessed relief as we took our places in the seats on the Florida train. We were on our way to Heaven —beloved, beautiful Florida, where the birds were singing, the fish were jumping, and the flowers were blooming, and where, best of all, there was no snow.

Changes   The 1940's brought many changes.

They brought recurrent illness and a decree from my doctor that I must spend my winters in a warmer climate. The older children were grown, Margaret had married, Laird graduated from college, and Stephen was away at Prep School, so it was possible to make new plans and to change the pattern of our lives. The doctor's edict meant enforced trips to the south for three months or longer each winter, which served to initiate me into a better love and understanding of our country.

Teamwork: Husband and Wife   Many couples, if both are creative, work together on the same project. The book or painting becomes a joint expression of two personalities, although, in some cases, one, the stronger, is apt to predominate.

In the case of Arthur Covey and myself, we started unevenly. He was already a skilled professional artist while I was a student. He began as my teacher and felt it his duty to train, guide, and teach me. I benefited for many years from his generous help. When I first knew him, I worked on *his* projects, following his instructions. I did as I was told. After our marriage, this relationship continued. He was the teacher, I was the pupil. While this was going on, I was at the same time struggling to arrive at a personal expression of my own, un-dominated by him. It was not easy, because of the force of his personality.

Arthur Covey was a devoted, dedicated artist and mural painter. Coming from humble, unpromising and unsympathetic rural surroundings, he had somehow followed an instinctive creative urge, managed to put himself through art school in Chicago and found work that was congenial to him, work that he loved. He devoted himself to it wholeheartedly, with great singleness of purpose, executing many handsome mural commissions during the course of his long life. He had no hobbies and few side interests. He lived for his work and his work alone. He lived at the right time, enjoyed a national reputation and a wide appreciation of his work, and never knew what failure meant. Nor did he live to see his own type of work outmoded by changing conditions.

During my apprenticeship, while I was striving to be a painter, his advice and help were invaluable. He took a keen interest in every phase of my development. This continued even after I wrote my earliest books, for I was still assisting him in his painting projects. (We did one joint mural project, a set of King Arthur Panels, and another set of nursery rhymes, for the Children's Orthopedic Hospital in Orange, New Jersey, in the early twenties.) With the writing of *Phebe Fairchild, Her Book,* (1936), my first historical book, however, I became primarily an author, using my art as an accessory to my writing and not as a creative expression in itself. I was no longer a painter.

This development into the writing field took me out from under Arthur Covey's influence. I was no longer his pupil, I was going in a new direction—a direction in which he could not follow, to guide me. I remember that he made a few helpful suggestions when I was revising the manuscript of *Phebe Fairchild, Her Book,* but never for any book after that. He did not know or understand the writer's problems. So I had to make my way alone.

He took little or no interest in my successive books, although he was generous enough to admire my work when it was brought to his attention. He was proud of my books and the reputation I was making in the writing field, and when talking to friends, took a great deal of credit, and rightly, for my training and the help he had given me as a student. But in the books themselves he had little or no interest. Many of them he never saw or read. Publication day for a new book, always a red-letter day for me, meant nothing to him.

I had learned in the early days to keep my work outwardly unimportant. I never talked about it in the family—there were some exceptions, of course—I wanted to avoid contributing to a feeling of jealousy. In fact, I learned that it was a wise policy never to talk about my work even to friends and acquaintances, unless questions were first asked me. I never liked the idea of boasting or bragging about my achievements —it was contrary to my nature. So my books developed independently, somewhat "under cover."

There were other reasons for this, besides a desire on my part never to be boastful. Arthur Covey never had the same interest in children that I did, and did not understand them or their needs; so he would not have been able to sense how important books were in filling those needs, or which concepts put into books could best do this. This province was entirely beyond his scope. I could not bear to have a cherished idea of mine thoughtlessly condemned and trampled underfoot. So I found it better not to share it at all.

A good example of this basic difference is shown in the case of Margaret's children. Mr. Covey was a doting, possessive father and grandfather, and automatically took the two boys under his roof in their time of need. I wanted them, too, but before I could agree to taking them, I had to get a promise from him that there would be no spankings or physical punishment, and that all disciplining would be left to me. His ideas of handling a child and mine were radically different. This arrangement worked out well to our and the boys' benefit.

Then, too, during the years when my Regionals were developing, Arthur Covey was at the peak of his mural painting career and his work absorbed him completely. He had little time or inclination to share my creative interests or to wonder specifically, what was going on in the little brown studio at the edge of the hayfield. He simply did not bother his head about it! He often had a capable male assistant working with him for extended periods, and my chief concern and duty was to see that the two men were kept well-fed at repeated intervals and that the housework ran smoothly and efficiently.

So we learned to go along happily each in his own way, each doing work he loved and each respecting the other.

PROFESSIONAL 1940's AND 1950's

Childhood of the Present On my trips south I saw the real America for the first time. I saw and learned what the word *region* meant as I witnessed firsthand different ways of life unlike my own. What interested me most was the way the children were living. I saw them first in Louisiana, then in Florida and the North Carolina mountains, leading lives completely different from the children in Connecticut, and I wondered why no one had taken the trouble to point out these differences. We had plenty of books that tell how children live in Alaska, Holland, China, and Mexico, but no books at all telling about the many ways children live here in the United States. Why shouldn't the children of Ohio and Connecticut have stories to read of the exciting lives of children in Louisiana, Florida, and the North Carolina mountains? There must be other unknown ways of life in other parts of the country, too, if an author could and would only seek them out. These questions gave me no rest and resulted in the beginning of this series.

Through the writing of my Regional books I gained a certain insight into childhood of today, realizing how today's fast-moving pace and strains and stresses were shaping children's lives in ways that contrast vividly with childhood of the past.

Generalized statements about children are usually only half-truths, because of their great individuality. My experiences put me in close touch with many individual children, all, in no matter what class of society or economic bracket, or in what environment, with definite problems to face. Each, a person in his own right, must meet life in his own way. Some get far too little help from adults and have to struggle alone. The life of any one of them is worth recording.

My choice of locations has never been arbitrary. I have not, for instance, put my finger on a certain spot on the map of the United States and said, "There! I will go there to write a Regional book!" Some of the locations have been chosen by invitation, some without, some with the help of good friends, and some by sheer accident, the felicitous accident that brings us to places we know we were meant to find. I believe I have been "led" to the location of many of my stories. These locations reflect a variety of pattern in family life, environment, background, climate, and occupation. I have found no lack of story or drama in any one region.

In the earlier years, convenience was a factor in my choice. At first, I wrote of those regions to which my travels took me twice a year, en route from Connecticut to Florida and back. After the Regional series became better known, I went to a number of locations—Arkansas, South Dakota, Iowa, Vermont, and California—by special invitation of children living there, who knew my books and begged to be written about. Each region brought its own appeal and offered unique drama of its own. In all the regions I visited, I never failed to receive the complete cooperation of both children and adults. They were thrilled to help me in every way possible.

The Regionals were begun after I had spent some seven years on historical research for my historical books. I had reached a point where I was tired of trying to recreate life secondhand, getting material from secondhand sources. This work done in my isolated studio or in a library alcove was too confining and narrow. It offered no opportunity for growth. I wanted to get out and see people and get to know them. Then maybe I could write about them.

During this transition period away from historical research into real-life research, my first impulse was always to go to the library and "read up" about a region. The WPA American Guide series of books for certain states had some useful material, but often even in these, I could not find the detailed, specific information I needed. I soon learned that one week spent in the region was more helpful than six weeks even in the best library, reading secondhand and generalized information with the human side left out. What I wanted was detailed day-to-day living of human beings. I wanted facts, but facts as they related to people. I could get this only by going to the place itself.

Coming into a new region by car—for instance, the peanut farm region of eastern North Carolina and southern Virginia —my curiosity was immediately aroused by the rows of strange-looking haystacks lined up across the fields, unlike any that I had ever seen before. So we stopped and I asked questions: "What are the haystacks? How do you grow peanuts? Do you use a threshing machine? Who grows them? Where do they live? Do the children help? What is that funny-looking two-wheeled cart used for?" I wanted to know specifically how the people on a peanut farm made a living from their peanut crop. I remember well how when I stopped in unannounced at a "peanut" school and talked to the children there, an eleven-year-old boy held up his hand and said, "I've lived on a peanut farm all my life and I can tell you all about peanuts!" He *could* and *did*. His real name was Billy Ben, and my book was called *Peanuts for Billy Ben.*

Of each region, I wanted to know in what ways it was unique and peculiar to itself, unlike other regions. What kind of lives do the people live? Of a family, what is the father's occupation, what kind of house do they live in, what do they eat, what clothes do they wear, what is their speech like, their choice of words? What is the weather and climate and how do they adjust to it? What recreation, what social activities do they have, what ideals, how do they get along with their neighbors? What are the hazards, conflicts, problems in their way of life? Are they victims of their environment, or are they able to rise above it and control their own lives? What sad or happy things take place and how do these things affect them? All people, young and old, respond to a sympathetic listener, and soon the outward questions are no longer needed, they take me along voluntarily into the heart of their lives and share even those aspects they hold most dear. What a privilege it is to have earned their confidence! How unworthy one must always feel.

There was another transition to be made—the transition from the use of imaginary characters to real ones. In my historical books, while I was able to gather accurate outward details of child and family life of the past from records left in book form, my characters themselves had to be invented, and also many of their activities. Here, the author's imagination came into full play.

This practice was soon abandoned as I went direct to the setting of my story and met the people there face to face. I found myself choosing my characters from among them. They were there before me, alive and real, acting a play on a stage especially for my benefit. I saw the father of a family with indecisive manner, many faults and excuses, I saw the way he was dressed, I heard the words he used. I saw my little heroines, with their bright eyes and tangled hair, the clothes they wore, I listened to their eager tales. My characters came to life before my eyes. I no longer needed to invent them. And how much finer and richer and more satisfying were they than any fictional characters I might have dreamed up!

Certain authors and critics feel that characters and stories that come from the imagination are superior to those in real life; and they exalt the wonders and powers of the imagination. I would only say that the imagination has very definite limitations and cannot compete with reality; and that it takes imagination of the highest order to be able to enter the heart and mind of a stranger who is different from oneself. I made this transition easily, because I soon came to see what richness real life had to offer. I soon found it difficult, if not impossible, to go back to my former practice of inventing characters and situations.

Regional Experiences in Brief The many stories behind the Regionals—gathering the material and writing the books— are too long to be included here. Brief accounts from a few of the books can serve to suggest the richness of the entire regional experience to an author.

BAYOU SUZETTE 1943 For our first winter in the south, in 1941–2, we went to New Orleans. Stephen, then thirteen, was put into a private school, where he began to pick up French readily. Mr. Covey painted daily in the French Quarter and enjoyed the companionship of other artists there. I was working on the illustrations for *The Little Farm,* but spent part of my time in the library, studying the early history of New Orleans, in preparation for another historical book. On Saturdays we drove out into the country to explore, and soon my interests were deflected into a new direction.

It was in Louisiana that I first discovered Regional America, where I first found the little village of Lafitte on a bayou twenty miles south of Gretna. I found Lafitte and its people, who so fascinated and inspired me and kept me coming again and again, with sketchbook and notebook, to put down a tangible record of their lives, in what became my first Regional, *Bayou Suzette.* New Orleans and Louisiana opened my eyes to the great diversity of pattern in the ways of life of America, and helped me to forget my own life in thinking of others.

The setting was unique. The people, most of them speaking French, lived in small houses, each with its own dock and boats, facing the bayou, and many of their activities were carried on out-of-doors. Every aspect of their life was controlled by the bayou. What fun for the children, playing on the docks and on the winding levee-paths, in and out of boats, fishing, crabbing, mending nets, catching baby alligators, living and knowing the water, but living with danger, too, always distrustful and afraid, for alas, very few of them could swim.

After my husband and Stephen drove north in late March in our car, for the spring term of Stephen's Connecticut school, I stayed on in New Orleans. I was still far from well, unable to cope with the cold spring in the north. On three days a week, I hired a taxi-driver in Gretna to take me down to Lafitte in the morning, and to come back for me at 5 P.M., after I had spent a busy, tiring, but rewarding day. On alternating days I stayed in bed in town, to regain my strength for continuing trips.

I made many friends along the bayou and filled my sketchbook and notebooks with exciting story material, although I still had no idea what form the book would take nor what it would lead to. I can still remember my farewell to my bayou friends, in this my first region, and the pangs of heartache I felt as I took my leave.

STRAWBERRY GIRL 1945   The next winter we went to Florida, and here again a new way of life confronted me. One January day, while driving with friends through the Plant City area, we saw children and adults picking strawberries out in a field. Beside the road was a small stand filled with baskets of berries. A little girl with flaxen hair and a pert, inquisitive face, stood there, hoping to sell to passersby. We did not stop, but my friend said jokingly: "Why not write a book about raising strawberries? You could call it *Strawberry Girl!*"

We all laughed, but the idea struck home. I was ready to do it, but how? There was many difficulties in the way. The setting was not so unique and ready-made as the one in Louisiana had been. Strawberries were grown in many outlying areas. It was wartime, we had no car in Florida, there was no gas. I was unable to get to the country until I met a County Health nurse, with a gas allowance, who was making a maternity survey in the Cumbee section outside Lakeland. I rode with her, and while she was doing her work in various homes, I observed the interiors, listened to the local speech and studied character. I had to memorize my impressions, although in a few places I made sketches. I spent Saturday evenings milling through the crowds of country people in town to do their trading. On market days, I went to the Farmers Market, to talk to farmers and their wives, to ask them questions and take down their replies. Each Saturday, my husband and I went to a weekly stock auction a mile out of town to sketch. It was an exciting experience, watching the horses, cows, mules, and hogs being auctioned off to the highest bidder. The original "Shoestring," in black felt Cracker hat, ushered the animals in and out of the ring. And there in the audience sat the real "Birdie Boyer"—just waiting to be put into a book!

The "strawberry schools" were closed during January, February, and March, so the children could pick berries. I sat on my campstool in the bright sun, sketching them as they picked, and listening to their songs and chatter. Somehow, all these miscellaneous ideas and impressions fused themselves into a dramatic plot and made a book—my second Regional.

BLUE RIDGE BILLY 1946 In the spring of 1945, returning from Florida to Connecticut, we stopped for six weeks in Ashe County, North Carolina. Gas rationing was still in force, we had no car with us, so we had to hitchhike on trips to the country with the county school superintendent and others. I found plenty of story material and Mr. Covey loved the mountains for painting and did some fine watercolors.

That fall, on our way south we stopped again at Huckleberry Mountain, south of Asheville, and Mr. Covey wanted to spend the winter there. Stephen came by train on his Christmas holiday to join us, but it turned out to be "the coldest winter in fifty years"! I did get many sketches and had many contacts with the mountain children and their parents. Wherever I went, I was impressed with the singularity of the mountain character—the unreasonable domination of the tyrannical father, the subservience of his wife, and the meekness of the repressed children, whose parents had not the desire nor the knowledge of how to let them grow up being themselves. The mountain children clearly showed their Scotch-Irish heritage, with their beautiful, almost beatific faces, their shy and wistful smiles, and the predominance of redheads among them. They did not know how to play—even on snowy days, they had no sleds, and never thought of making shift with boards for sliding. They were surprisingly lacking in inventive play and ingenuity. Yet their very lacks made them all the more appealing.

Stephen did a fine piece of interviewing for me here, at the age of fifteen. I very much wanted to visit a particular family, who lived up on top of a mountain, practically inaccessible to *me*. Stephen climbed up the precipitous slope on his own, visited the family, and brought me a wonderful report, as detailed as if I had made the trip myself. Instinctively he had sensed and been able to draw out from this strange family many of the details of their life that I wanted to know.

After an enjoyable but chilly Christmas, completely snowbound and cut off from the world, Stephen returned by train to his Pennsylvania school, and we went on to Florida—to get warm.

JUDY'S JOURNEY 1947 Through my reading I had developed a deep concern for the migrants, for the hordes of children always "on the go" helping to pick our crops. A Florida friend had seen women and children leaving Florida by night in canvas-covered trucks, starting northward, driven by crop recruiters from the north. The Home Missions Council of the National Council of Churches in America made it possible for me to do my field work in migrant camps in New Jersey.

There I saw and talked to migrant families, both Negro and Anglo-white, from many different areas. Some worked in nearby fields picking beans for a large freezing corporation, and others in the packing houses. I visited children in a child care center, cabins at the camps, and often out in the fields where they were picking.

At the camps, the squalor in which the children were living was sickening, although they were unconscious of it. Those of school age were given real responsibility. They had to get supper ready, beds made, and ironing done, while their parents were out in the field. They carried cans of coal-oil or jugs of water, loaves of bread or firewood. In one camp all the preschool children had been left in the care of an aged, helpless man who could not get out of his wheelchair. Many poignant experiences preceded the writing of this book.

COTTON IN MY SACK 1949   The children in Yarbro School, near Blytheville, Arkansas, invited me to come to write about them. This was the first of many such invitations. When I told the children that I knew nothing about cotton or how it was grown, they assured me they would help and help they did, for the book is more theirs than mine. I made two visits to Arkansas, one in the spring for the planting and a longer one in the fall for the picking. I interviewed more than twenty-five families, sharecroppers, tenants, and owners, to listen to their respective points of view. The housing for the sharecroppers was unspeakably bad and the conditions under which the children lived most depressing. But the children were alert and responsive, hungry for love and understanding, and I came to love them dearly. They shared all the sorrow and tragedy of their lives with me, as freely as the little joy and happiness. The story of my experiences in the cotton country is too long to be told here, but it was a rich and rewarding one.

The big event of the 1940's was the award of the Newbery Medal to *Strawberry Girl* in 1946. No one was more astonished than I to receive it. Had it been given to my book

Indian Captive, the Story of Mary Jemison, which I considered my major and most scholarly work, I would not have been surprised. I had envisioned a series of Regional books, for I knew there were many regions little known and neglected in children's books. The series was barely started, and I had already daringly broken down a few unwritten taboos, I had written more plainly and realistically than other children's authors, I had taken my material and my characters direct from real life instead of from the imagination, and my Regionals were not yet entirely accepted or approved. I was an innovator and a pioneer in a new direction, and I knew I had a long and difficult task ahead to earn the acceptance which I was not expecting so soon. But the award focused national attention on *Strawberry Girl* and the books to follow, so I was very grateful.

The convention of the American Library Association was held at Buffalo that year, and at the various meetings and receptions, I received invitations from librarians to go to many parts of the country—Seattle, Utah, California, Kansas, Texas, Oklahoma, Minnesota—to write about their region. Afterwards, the award brought much publicity, including requests for personal interviews and radio appearances, for personal appearances at libraries and schools, most of which I was unable to accept. Those that I did accept were strenuous and wearing, and I was glad when the flurry subsided, and I could retire to private life again.

An entire book could be written about my experiences in other regions during the 1950's—in San Angelo, Texas, for *Texas Tomboy,* in Perry, Oklahoma, for *Boom Town Boy,* in McLaughlin, South Dakota, for *Prairie School,* in Remsen, Iowa, for *Corn Farm Boy,* and other places. The list goes on and on, always a new environment and way of life to be studied, and always good people who shared the intimacy of their lives with me, each region more exciting and stimulating than the last, each region calling for one's deepest powers of observation, understanding, and compassion.

A side hobby for many years was my interest in children's own creative work. Through the summers of the 1940's and 1950's, I held painting classes for children in my studio at Greenacres, and also in Florida in the winter months. The children painted on large sheets of newsprint, kneeling or sitting on the floor. Their paintings were large, brilliant in color, and exciting in subject matter. I kept my walls covered with examples of their work, found great inspiration in them and never tired of them. Working with the children, many of them of preschool age, trying to stimulate their natural expression was as valuable an experience for me as for them. To see a frustrated child shake off his fears and inhibitions and create freely and joyously is like watching a tight flower bud open and expand in the warm glow of the sunlight. It has always given me great happiness.

After *Strawberry Girl* won the Newbery Medal, children from a school in Toledo, Ohio, sent me a number of beautiful murals which they had made to illustrate various books of mine. These decorated the high walls of my studio for twenty years and never lost their fresh virility and beauty. I helped several local groups to paint murals from my Regionals, which in turn found places on my walls. My present studio in Florida is hung with many beautiful examples of children's paintings, including a life-size figure of Birdie Boyer, painted in 1946 by an Ohio girl of ten years.

The Roundabout America Books

"Come, let us look at the ways of life
in our country. Let us go into out-of-the-way
corners, up on the hills and down in the
valleys, into city streets and village homes.
Let us see and get to know the people.
Here and there, roundabout America, are friends
worth knowing."

This invitation introduced third and fourth graders to my *Roundabout America* series, begun in 1952. Teachers asked me for shorter and easier stories to fill the gap between my picture books and the Regionals. Because they, too, are regional in character, utilizing leftover material from the older books, they become stepping stones to the Regionals. As a group, the *Roundabout America* books present vivid glimpses of many diversified ways of life in our country—orange grove, piney woods, Negro quarter, fishing village, peanut farm, housing project, penthouse, city slum, cranberry bog, island, locks, and riverbank life, Indian reservation, chicken farm, cotton farm, tree farm, sheep farm, Navaho hogan, Spanish village, ghost mining-town, and high-rise city apartment.

During the fifties and sixties, I began writing poems, hymns, and songs, collaborating with Clyde Robert Bulla for the music. These were first regional songs for the inarticulate children I wrote about, who could not do it themselves. Their need for expression stirred up my instinct and love of poetry, which due to editorial advice on my first book, had long been buried. I wrote a book of hymns for children, a book of city songs, then poems began to go into my picture books and the *Roundabout America* books. One of my very first poems, *People,* from *Skipping Village,* was reprinted innumerable times over the years. This fact gave me the courage to collect all my poems into one volume, *The Life I Live: Collected Poems,* published in a beautiful format by Walck in 1965. It is "the happiest of all my books." The writing of my poems has been one of my greatest joys.

The Practical Side   I am often asked about the practical side of making a book.

If it is a picture book, I make sketches in a "dummy"—a blank book of the size intended—as I have already described. I color the sketches in this dummy, to show the number of printings necessary. The dummy is submitted to the editor, who may or may not suggest changes. When the approved dummy is returned to me, I draw the illustrations on 3-ply bristol board, making them one-third larger than page size. All drawings are improved by reduction. I make color overlays to show the placement of the colors; I do not make color separations, as many artists do. I provide printed, not painted, color samples for the printer to follow. I always design the title page, cover, and jacket and use hand lettering.

For books for older children, the process is different.

As soon as I return from a region, I have a big job to do. I have to copy all the notes I have taken, classifying them under various headings, making them readily and quickly accessible. Then I make an outline for my story, listing the various incidents I wish to include under the different chapter headings. I write my text in longhand first, and often revise it in longhand, then revise again as I type it. (The subject has, of course, been approved by the editor in advance.) I send the typed manuscript in, to be read and approved, copyedited (improving or disapproving of my punctuation!) and sent to the printer to be set into type. If any changes are suggested by the editor, the manuscript or portions of it may be returned to me for this purpose. If any changes in format are contemplated, I am always consulted. For many years, with Lippincott, I worked directly with the head of the manufacturing department in planning all details of type and format. It was in this way that a beautiful format was devised for the Regionals.

While the manuscript is at the printers, while I am waiting for the galley proofs, having kept a carbon of the manuscript, I am working on the illustrations. For the Regionals, these are graphite pencil drawings on 3-ply bristol board, and are reproduced by high-light halftone offset. The drawings for the Roundabouts are ink drawings, reproduced by letterpress.

When the galley proofs reach me, two sets are sent, one for me to read and correct, and to answer editorial or printers' queries; the other set for me to cut up and paste into a blank dummy, allowing space on the proper page for each illustration, of which I usually make about fifty.

After I wrap up a large package containing original manuscript, the original illustrations, corrected galley proofs, and the printer's dummy and ship it to the publishers, my work on a book is finished. The rest is up to the publisher. I see and hear nothing more until months later, when a book package arrives out of the blue, containing the first copy, hot off the press, for me to hold in my hands and marvel at. There is no other thrill so great for an author-illustrator as seeing the first copy of a book he has labored over and believed in and deeply loved.

LATER YEARS

PERSONAL AND PROFESSIONAL

In the early fifties, I was very ill again. Due to an unsuspected allergy, I lost thirty pounds in weight, which also added to my exhaustion. I could not take even short rides in the car for many months. Having to spend so much time lying down, it was during this period that I started writing verse again.

One of the best cures for pain, illness, and physical discomfort is creative thinking. It fills one with a sense of well-being, an indescribable joy which carries one's thoughts and imagination along, so that one's body can be forgotten. Creative effort lifts one above the senses of the corporeal body. It is in periods like these that I have come to realize that work is a sacred thing, a way to praise God.

It was in the fifties that, through help of good friends, the Glenn Abernethys whose daughters loved my books, I was led to a dedicated doctor in North Carolina. Through the magic of modern medicine, cures then only recently discovered for pernicious anemia, I was restored to active life again. Previously I had had to give up driving a car, working in my garden and many other forms of physical activity. Now, I "got up and walked again." I had lived a miracle.

Each return to Florida gladdened my heart. The very sunlight had a psychological effect on me and always gave me a great lift. We built a home in Florida in 1951, and after that our treks were simplified. We now had a place where we could keep easels, canvases, stretchers, paintboxes, books, papers, reference material, and all the supplies needed by two artists. We no longer had to cart them back and forth in a loaded-down car. We kept ample supplies at both ends of the road, so we could travel more lightly.

We bought a second-hand car in Florida to keep there, leaving our old one in Connecticut. This meant we could give up the long tiresome drives and go by train. My husband loved train travel and was reluctant to give it up and start flying, until poor health and a lack of energy made the latter really necessary. I made my first flight to Iowa in 1946 and was converted to the air immediately. In the years that followed, with all the traveling I had to do, flying took all the wear and tear out of it for me, and I indulged in it continuously. Many trips would not have been possible for me without flying.

My husband loved the old farm in Connecticut and even after the children had left home, and the care and upkeep of it became a burden to us both, he was reluctant to part with it. He had at first resented his winters in Florida, feeling cut off there from his professional contacts in New York, but he gradually came to see how greatly the easier winters benefited his health, and to love Florida very much. But he insisted on spending at least six months each summer at Greenacres, where he could be near the children and his grandchildren.

The summers were happy ones, with the children coming and going, often large crowds over weekends playing badminton and croquet and eating picnic suppers out on the lawn. There were periods when I had help in the house or when Mr. Covey could stay with the married children, that gave me the freedom to make a regional visit to some part of the country. Sometimes, now, looking back, I wonder how I ever squeezed these visits in.

The new home in Florida gave us great happiness. We found two waterfront lots with a fisherman's storage building on them. We added a large studio at each end, one for Mr. Covey and one for me, and turned the original building into a tiny living room and dining-kitchen area. I took great pride and delight in my magic kitchen, which I had planned in careful detail. Everything was within arm's reach, quite a contrast to the old farm kitchen in Connecticut, which had necessitated so much "leg work." We each had our own privacy. At his end of the house, Mr. Covey could still stretch large canvases, splash oil paint and spill turpentine. He worked on his major mural commission, the ceiling paintings for Trinity Lutheran Church at Worcester, Massachusetts, during the early 1950's in this room. At my end of the house, with door closed, I could pound on my typewriter for long hours undisturbed.

There were other allures, the chief one being the beautiful outdoors. Within a short walk, Mr. Covey could find boats of all sizes, shapes, and colors, some under construction, some "on the ways" awaiting repair—all tantalizing material for drawings and paintings. He never tired of the scene or lost his skill in portraying it. Many of his finest watercolors were Florida subjects. Across the waterfront of our lots was an eighty-foot dock over a bayou, where fish leaped and sunshine danced on the waters.

Here, in sub-tropical Florida, I had the great happiness of building a year-round tropical garden, with two lath-houses filled with exotic plants from many parts of the world, none of which I had known in the north. A new way of gardening had to be learned, a real challenge in meeting extremes of heat and cold, of moisture and drought, but which when met, gave continuing year-round beauty and satisfaction. I have taken great pleasure in the creative aspects of gardening, for I feel one can create beauty with plants as well as on paper, with words, pencil, or paint. After Stephen's encouragement, I surprised myself by starting to drive our car again, even passing the test to get a new driver's license. Soon I had to take over all the driving, and I enjoyed it much more than I had in earlier years. Life in Florida in the winters continued to be rich and full. Many of the pressures of earlier years had lessened, and as Mr. Covey and I had both won praise and recognition in our chosen fields, we could work more leisurely, savoring each moment to the full.

Various awards have come over the years, for which I am humbly grateful. In 1943, *Bayou Suzette* won the Ohioana Medal. After the Newbery Medal for *Strawberry Girl, Judy's Journey* received the 1947 Child Study Association Award. In 1969 came the Regina Medal from the Catholic Library Association (given for books which portray spiritual values) and also the University of Southern Mississippi Children's Collection Medallion. There have been honorary degrees from Wartburg College, Iowa, University of North Carolina, Capital University, Ohio, and Southwestern College, Kansas. But the awards that have touched me most deeply are the words of the children, who have, often inarticulately, told me in letters how dearly loved my books have become to them.

Stephen's army service took him to Germany, where he was given congenial work to do supervising a Craft Center for soldiers. After he had served his allotted time, he stayed on of his own volition, at a fixed salary, enough to live on. In Amsterdam he met a Dutch girl, Yolanthe de Raadt, to whom he was married in 1955. Yolanthe was a lovely, vivacious girl, full of life and spirit, with a knowledge of four languages, and as Mr. Covey said, "a welcome addition to the Covey tribe!"

Their first child, Michael, was born in Stuttgart in April, 1956. This made me a true grandmother. Stephen's second child was a girl! To have a girl in the Covey family was a real event. The daughter that I had always longed for became a granddaughter. (My stepchildren's children had all been boys, Margaret's three and Laird's one.) So we were all thrilled and excited. Annual visits to Phoenix, Arizona, where Stephen later found work to his liking and built a home of his own, soon became routine for me. In 1964, another little Covey girl, Jeanine, was born. This made me rich, with two granddaughters and one grandson of my own.

In 1967, I adopted my stepson Laird. I remember many years ago when Stephen was small, a friend said to me, "Of course, a stepson is never the same as your own son, your own flesh and blood." I was taken aback, for the idea was new to me. I turned to her then and said, "To me, there is no difference. Laird has been my son since he was four." And now I can add, "No stepson could ever be a better son than Laird has been to me." He has needed no formal adoption.

In 1958–60, Mr. Covey was very ill. After a long life of perfect health, with seldom even a cold to trouble him, he did not take readily to invalidism. In the Florida sunshine he could rest out-of-doors, and after many months he began to improve. The first sign of better health was getting back to his painting again. He brought out a book full of sketches he had made in Arizona in 1956 and started some watercolors, paintings that still showed the touch of the master.

One day, February 4, 1960—he told me how well he felt, and I went into his studio to look at the bold, vigorous drawing on his easel. I knew how happy he was to be back at his beloved work again, after all the months of enforced idleness.

"I'll finish it tomorrow!" he said.

But the painting was never finished. That night he died in his sleep. After nearly forty years together, our companionship was ended. He had had a good life, and his work was done.

Life was simpler now—I was alone. I still went to Greenacres for the summers, only three months instead of six. Although I still loved the place as Mr. Covey had loved it, I knew I had to give it up, for the care and upkeep had become a real burden to me. I had had the full responsibility for it for years before his death. I spent two summers clearing out the contents of his studio and finding a depository for a record of his life's work. Then I began on my own—the little brown studio at the edge of the hayfield. I started to assemble my manuscripts and the other multitudinous materials connected with my work, and to distribute them to a number of libraries, most of them in universities, who had begun collecting my work.

The long years of rich family life in the big house on the hundred green acres came to an end. Margaret, my step-daughter, died at the age of fifty-five, two years after her father's death. Because Laird and Stephen decided they could not use the place, in 1964 I sold the house and my studio to a young New England couple with children growing up—the Irving Nortons—who became the fourth family living there. The Covey chapter was over and a new one had begun.

What is in store for the old house at Greenacres? That it will be lived in and enjoyed by people who will love it as we loved it, is my only hope. The old house had seen three families come and go. It had seen joy and sorrow, happiness and tragedy, it had witnessed all the vicissitudes of human experience. It stands a monument to its creators.

> *They built well, who built it,*
> *The old house there by the roadside.*
>
> *The winds blew cold against it,*
> *The snows of winter beat on*
> *and pounded it,*
>
> *The winds went whistling*
> *through the chimney,*
> *Whistled loud enough to*
> *chill one's blood.*
>
> *The rains and storm buffeted it,*
> *But never reached its heart,*
> *its heart of warmth and love.*

The old house stands stiff and staunch
close by the roadside.
They built well, who built it.

Now my home is in Florida. As I have said so many, many times, on each return from another part of the country: I am happy to come back to Florida, to peace and sunshine. Here, where the birds are singing, the fish are jumping, and the flowers are blooming, here I have put down my roots and made my chosen home.

"A carpet of green, cool depths of shade;
A burst of color that paint never made.
Gay pattern of vine or stem or leaf,
Tender new growth stands out in relief.

A sea of loveliness, a world of its own,
Inside the gate I wander alone;
Here peace and joy and deep content,
*Here tranquillity to me is sent."**

* "My Garden," from *The Life I Live: Collected Poems.* Walck, 1965.

INDEX